THE
CONFIDENCE KIT

Caroline Foran is a Number One bestselling
author, freelance lifestyle journalist and
co-founder of digital publishing venture
GAFFInteriors.ie.

Caroline lives in Dublin and prior to her career in
media, she obtained a degree in Communications
and a master's in Film & Television Studies, both
from Dublin City University.

Her first book, *Owning It: Your Bullsh*t-Free
Guide to Living with Anxiety,* was published in
2017. *The Confidence Kit* is her second book.

The
Confidence
Kit

CAROLINE FORAN

HACHETTE
BOOKS
IRELAND

Cataloguing in Publication Data is available from the British Library

ISBN 9781473677173

Typeset in Neutraface Slab Text, 10.5 pt by grahamthew.com

Excerpt from Brag!: *The Art of Tooting Your Own Horn without Blowing It* by
Peggy Klaus, copyright © 2003. Reprinted by permission of Grand Central
Publishing, an imprint of Hachette Book Group, Inc.
Excerpt from *How to Be a Stoic: Using Ancient Philosophy to Live a Modern Life*
by Massimo Pigliucci, copyright © 2017. Reprinted by permission of Basic Books,
an imprint of Perseus Books, LLC, a subsidiary of Hachette Book Group, Inc.

Printed and bound in Great Britain by Clays Ltd, St Ives plc
Hachette Books Ireland policy is to use papers that are natural, renewable
and recyclable products and made from wood grown in sustainable forests.
The logging and manufacturing processes are expected to conform to the
environmental regulations of the country of origin.

Hachette Books Ireland
8 Castlecourt Centre
Castleknock
Dublin 15, Ireland

A division of Hachette UK Ltd
Carmelite House, 50 Victoria Embankment, EC4Y 0DZ

www.hachettebooksireland.ie

Contents

For Bear, who keeps me company while
I write and cuddles me after I've done
something that scares me.

Introduction

What this book will do for you

DISCLAIMER: This is not a book to read if your aim is to become entirely 'fearless'. I am not, unfortunately, a custodian of a long-kept secret that will forever rid you of all your fears and leave you with the confidence of a lion, strutting his or her stuff with a Kanye-like swagger among the African plains.

Fearlessness is not the goal.

Expecting yourself to never feel fear is as futile as expecting yourself to go through life without experiencing stress. If that's your aim, I wish you luck but I cannot help you. Instead, I will help you to work with fear, and learn to build confidence. We can employ specific strategies that help our fear work for us rather than against us. We cut the bullsh*t.

ANOTHER DISCLAIMER: Opening a book entitled *The Confidence Kit*, you're likely to assume that the person who wrote it is bursting with self-confidence. The kind of person who jumps out of aeroplanes with the same ease that you order your morning Americano. Right? Wrong. But wait. Don't close the cover just yet.

In the interest of transparency, let it be known that the focus of this book is not on the immediate right-here-right-now fear you'd feel if you were standing in front of an axe murderer – that's not a fear you want to get rid of – but, rather, perceived fears, one of which is the fear of failure, that hold us back from pursuing our goals and feeling confident.

On the subject of transparency, I feel fear – more specifically, the perceived fear of failure – greatly. My self-confidence has been known to pool around my ankles on many an occasion, which might, on a separate note, explain why I've been cursed with cankles all these years.

But let's just ruminate for a moment: let's assume you've picked up this book because you want to become a more confident and courageous person. You're fed up with the fear that holds you back. Well, how could you expect to learn the skills of managing your fear – personal, social or professional – from someone who's never felt the faintest flutter of it? That's like learning how to be a pilot from someone who's read the manual but never actually flown the plane. So, rest assured, I'm right there with you in the cockpit. Being familiar with fear is step one on the road to building your confidence.

In the interest of clarity, it's worth knowing that this is my second book. Maybe my first book, *Owning It: Your Bullsh*t-Free Guide To Living With Anxiety*, enjoys permanent residency on your bedside shelf. Or maybe you've never heard of it – or me, for that matter – but you liked the colours of this book's cover enough to pick it up. (I don't blame you; whoever said we shouldn't judge a book by its cover?) Regardless of *how* you've arrived here, allow me a little room to ramble to ensure that we're all on the same page (yes, pun intended).

My first foray as an author spoke directly to those grappling with anxiety across the full spectrum – from the mild, where you may be prone to bouts of worry, to the extreme, where you temporarily cease to function. The latter was my experience, once upon a time, and it was precisely how I dealt with it that formed the basis of my first book. To mirror a concept (which has been a great source of inspiration for me) put forward by motivational speaker Zig Ziglar in his book *Over The Top*[1], *Owning It* chronicled my path from survival to stability – or, more specifically, from merely existing between panic attacks to feeling well on a daily basis.

This book is the next organic step, informed, again, by my own experiences. Having arrived at a point of stability, the safe ground of my comfort zone, I know that true success, which can come in many forms, lies beyond, on not-so-safe ground and far outside my comfort zone. While I may have a firm grasp on the acute anxiety that controlled me for so long, my confidence as a person out and about in the world, wanting to achieve things, needed work.

Evolving as I do, this book casts its net a little wider and reaches beyond 'anxiety sufferers'. It speaks to those among us who've come face to face with one of the less-than-favourable tenets of the human experience: fear. And, unless you've removed your brain's amygdala, that's just about everybody.

This book is about thriving in spite of your fear because if, like me, you're the proud proprietor of a pulse, you must accept that fear and anxiety are going to come along for the ride. What you'll learn, however, is that fear and confidence are two sides of the same coin – and it's up to you which side wins out.

From surviving to thriving is the most challenging path and one that, for many, is fraught with uncertainty, self-doubt and fear. In keeping with Ziglar's thinking, this is the path that takes us from stability to success.

The final stage in Ziglar's path takes us from success to significance ... This is a jump that I'm still figuring out.

You'll have to let me get back to you on that one.

I should say at the outset that reading *Owning It* is not a prerequisite for reading this book – this is not *Lord of the Rings: The Two Towers* – neither is having anxiety. If you did read my first book and you've mastered the art of managing your anxiety on a day-to-day basis, sitting comfortably at a point of stability, you will find that with *The Confidence Kit*, we're expanding our comfort zones and refining our skills, so that our lives are not defined by the absence of anxiety or any other uncomfortable experience, but by our ability to excel and enjoy success. It's the same way that good health is not simply defined by the *absence* of disease or infirmity, but by the *presence* of vitality and being in a state of complete mental, physical and social well-being; I need to eat well and exercise, nurturing my body and mind so that I can function at an optimum level. I apply the same logic to personal growth.

Whatever your experiences thus far, the only assumption here is that we all meet at a point of relative stability, with a collective yearning to move forward towards success, whatever this is for you – maybe it's giving a speech at a friend's wedding or getting the promotion you've been dreaming of. Together, we are lacking in the self-confidence necessary to pursue our own definition of success, while our fears stand in the way, giving us the middle finger. Dickheads.

Before diving into what this book can do for you, I'd like to give you a brief catch-up on how I arrived at this point.

Back in 2014, where *Owning It* starts, despite having had 'everything going for me', I fell to the floor with anxiety (both figuratively *and* literally). I had a significant breakdown brought on by rather insignificant events spanning several difficult months that would have an enormous impact on my lifestyle, and forever leave its marks – among them, a tendency towards near-constant catastrophic thinking (bad) and a bestselling book (not so bad). My challenge then was to get my head above water; to function as a 'normal' human being and do the more simple things, like leave the house without the crippling fear of a panic attack. I wanted to change my relationship with anxiety so that it no longer defined the parameters of my life. My goal was simple: I had to get back to basics, to reduce the feelings – both physical and emotional – of anxiety that plagued me constantly, to sleep through the whole night, to socialise without the need to flee and, ultimately, to *understand* rather than *fear* my body's stress response.

Having reached the point of stability where I could resume normal daily life with relative ease – one massive roadblock overcome – I was then approached with an opportunity of a lifetime: a book deal. The leap from stability to success beckoned. But when the initial disbelief and excitement – and prosecco – had worn off, I had to contend with a new set of anxieties, including, but not limited to, the following:

o 'Oh sh*t. What have you agreed to? Oh sh*t, sh*t, sh*t, SH*T. Can you really write a book?'
o 'Are you even a good writer?'
o 'Can you write this *particular* book when you still sometimes *feel* anxiety?'
o 'You're not a psychology professional, who are you to tell people how to manage their anxiety?'
o 'Should you not just carry on with your life instead of dredging all of this up?'
o 'Will anxiety define you again?'
o 'Will it be any good?'
o 'Will it be sh*t? Yes, it will probably be sh*t.'
o 'What will people think of you?'
o 'What if your anxiety comes back?'

And so the internal inquisition went on and on and on, demanding my attention most often between the hours of two and four a.m., when my rational, higher-thinking brain was busy resting and my irrational, child-like brain was bouncing off the walls.

Long story short, I wanted to get through it, so I did. I wrote it. It was tough and I was plagued with self-doubt, but I did it. When it was complete, it was a reward like no other. However, being me, my anxieties didn't end there. I realised I had a lot more to learn and a new set of skills to hone, which led nicely to book number two.

Along with the success of *Owning It* came a set of expectations that filled me with a new level of unease. Live national TV and radio, public-speaking appointments in front of hundreds of people, and all the while my anxious brain is shouting, 'But I have anxiety. Did you not read my book? I would rather eat my own arm than do all of this.'

In a relatively short space of time, I went from panic attacks on my sofa and a fear of leaving my house to facing what I, like so many others, had feared more than death itself: public speaking. Was I able for it? Gulp. And that's not to mention the fears and uncertainty around writing the follow-up book that you're reading right now – the process of which confirmed, for me, that second-album-syndrome is a very real thing. (FYI, the irony of having immense fear about writing a book about fear hasn't escaped me.)

But as I dealt with each one of these challenges, I found and developed techniques, tips and practices that helped me enormously. The more interviews and presentations and public-speaking events I did, the more my perceived fears began to shrink. Don't get me wrong, I still, on certain occasions, might want to regurgitate my breakfast at the thought of a broadcast interview or speaking on a podium to a group of people, but now I have perspective, understanding (around why my body behaves in this way) and, most importantly, experience.

In this book, I'll take you through the processes that I use so that I'm no longer afraid to say yes to challenges; something that helps my confidence massively. At the same time, there are occasions when I'm also no longer afraid to say no, which is important too. It's worth noting here that public speaking has certainly been a challenge for me, but for others it can be anything from going to a party to asking someone out on a date. The point is, it's all relative. Hopefully, with this book, you will be able to gain something that will enable you to push beyond the walls of your comfort zone to where success lies.

Up until the release of my first book, I had developed the skills necessary to live with anxiety, but the skills necessary to thrive outside of my comfort zone and my self-confidence in many areas needed work. I had a choice in any given situation: I could submit to the fear and stay comfortable in a cocoon of stability. I could say no to the second book offer, no to the presentations and talks I was being offered. That would be safe and easy.

Or, I could brace myself, take control and figure out a practical strategy for owning my fears, all of which would enable me to move closer to success. I could choose to stay behind my mental blocks or I could take them on. I chose the latter, and I'm guessing you will too.

That choice led to a toolkit, which continues to serve me well, and that toolkit is this book. *The Confidence Kit* takes the mental blocks that many of us are dealing with and turns them into building blocks with which you can work towards your version of success (something that depends on your own benchmarks, values and beliefs).

The thing about our fear response is that it's a non-negotiable part of us. For some, it's a major pain in the arse to manage, but by the final page of this book you'll believe it to be part of your success – so it's important to recognise it, own it and address it.

From this point, I have just one request: give up on trying to become fearless. Fearlessness is a false construct. Instead, accept fear as part of confidence. Contrary to popular belief and the physical effects that fear itself can manifest, fear does not negate courage. Nor does it negate confidence. Rather, it beckons it. The question is: Will you be paralysed by it or will you process it?

Will you own it?

A word about what to expect in terms of structure. *The Confidence Kit* is divided into three parts.

The first part explores precisely what fear is – for example, the difference between perceived fear and the fear you experience when you get a fright, why we fear failure and how fear works in our brains. Our fears aren't going anywhere so to really grow our confidence we need to embrace our fear and manage it.

I also look at what confidence is – and courage too – and why perfectionism can be a major roadblock on the road to achieving confidence, among other important topics. I tease apart the concept of the comfort zone and the other states of being that can help or hinder us. I distil the science and psychology surrounding all of this in as bullsh*t-free language as possible, with some expert input thrown in for good measure. Understanding all of this is essential and just as important as the specific confidence-building tools. Why? Because wrapping your head around exactly what you're dealing with – how it works and why it's normal – takes away a lot of the fear factor. For me, I always feel worse when I don't understand where it's coming from. This knowledge, however, puts you in control; it's empowering and a tool in itself.

In Part Two, we get right down to work with the strategies I use as often as is required to help me manage and own my fear. Here, I look at tools, such as 'fear hacking', 'sidestepping' and other tools that are available to us within stoicism and more. I have structured this part so that the tools are listed consecutively. You might decide to follow them in that same order – starting with 'goal-setting' and working through to 'repetition' and dealing with 'night gremlins' – but when you have a sense of things, you might dip in and out of the tools that speak most to you. There are no rules, and you won't always have to apply all of the tools at once. However, I strongly advise wrapping your head around the what and the why of Part One before tackling the toolkit itself.

For the toolkit, be prepared to do the work involved with a pen and paper (go out now and get yourself a trendy notebook) and be willing to take the action necessary to increase your self-confidence in particular areas of your life. The thing is, you can read all the books you want but until you get proactive in the face of fear, nothing will change.

Part Three wraps everything up with some crucial reminders to take forth with you. What if you fail? What should you do? How should you process that? And what if you succeed? Success is the goal but for many of us, we don't know quite what to do with it when we achieve it.

Looking at the contents page, it might seem overwhelming. The good news is, it's totally doable.

Ready to get to work?

PART ONE

LAYING THE FOUNDATIONS

The Comfort Zone

AH, 'THE COMFORT ZONE', a phrase with which every one of us is familiar. Is it a fixed thing? Absolutely not. Do many of us live our lives on the assumption that it is? Unfortunately, yes. Is the comfort zone a good thing or a bad thing? Well ... it's neither.

The comfort zone is nothing new, but understanding it is a very useful tool if your goal is to strategise a way out of it – or even just around it. The comfort zone was a concept put forward by psychologists Robert M. Yerkes and John D. Dodson after an experiment back in 1908, when they observed the ways in which a state of relative comfort could create a steady level of performance.

It has been defined as: a psychological and behavioural state in which we feel emotionally safe and at ease. In the comfort zone, we are anxiety-neutral. There is no fear, no risk, no stress and everything is familiar.

While I appreciate that daredevils and adrenaline junkies are the obvious outliers here, I can safely assume they're not reading this book. By and large, the rest of us live quite peacefully in the CZ and it's easy to see why; it's like one big Ugg boot.

The Yerkes-Dodson experiment

The most famous experiment on the comfort zone dates back to 1908 when Robert M. Yerkes and John D. Dodson examined the behaviours and performance of mice. In a small box, the mice were given a choice of entering a white or a black passage. The experimenters wanted the mice to enter the white passage and not the black, so when they went through the black one the mice were corrected by way of small electrical shocks which made them back-track and reconsider their choice. Yerkes and Dodson noticed that the mild shocks actually improved the mice's performance. Their ability to make the right decision sharpened. A slight increase in the shocks increased their performance – but only until a certain point, after which the mice's performances went downhill. A chart of the shock strength versus performance forms an inverted U. This inverted U shape became the standard – and somewhat simplistic – model for performance (of humans, not just mice) under stress. It is now widely accepted that, with no stress, performance is, generally speaking, steady (comfort zone). A little stress and performance generally improves. Too much, however, and it suffers. And we'll get to that more in a minute.[2]

Evolving from the moment we are born – shaping and reshaping, expanding or even shrinking with time and experience – your comfort zone is entirely relative to you and your beliefs, behaviours and life thus far. In this zone, you operate within the limitations of the skills and abilities you've already acquired, and you do so with almost no effort. In short, your comfort zone is what might be referred to as your 'norm'. For one person, public speaking or surfing a twenty-foot wave may well be within the realm of their comfort zone, whereas for someone else, a simple social encounter may take them completely outside their comfort zone; the latter was once how I felt.

Beyond the feeling of safety and familiarity, one of the most crucial defining characteristics of your comfort zone is that when you're in it, you feel as though you are in total control. You're in control of your emotions, your stress response and your physical body. You are not self-conscious. You function at a slow and steady pace, that isn't taxing on your mind or body. If you were to imagine your comfort zone as a line on a graph, it would have an even, steady rhythm and a gentle amplitude. There would be no major peaks or troughs.

Even though most descriptions of the comfort zone sound rather lovely, it's not always a happy place, and that is why it's sometimes referred to as 'the familiar zone'. The thing is, when we experience something repeatedly, it becomes familiar, but that does not necessarily mean the experience is a positive one. For example, you may become used to feeling lonely or disappointed or taken for granted. Obviously, this is a place from which you should want to break free so that you can live your life to the fullest, but sometimes it can become so familiar – and yes, comfortable – that you're not even aware of its negative impact on your well-being. This is a common problem when it comes to long-term romantic relation-ships that no longer serve us and why you might look at a friend in a toxic relationship and wonder how he or she doesn't see things as clearly as you do. Very often, they've come to accept it as their norm.

For the most part, we all want to stay within the bound-aries of our comfort zone. Who wouldn't? It's secure and easy. But there are some downsides to this. As described by Panicucci in 2007,[3] 'intellectual development and personal growth do not occur if there is no disequilibrium in a person's current thinking or feeling'. In other words, you can't achieve great success, whatever that may be to you, if you stay under the duvet, cosy as it is. With a little discomfort, as the Yerkes and Dodson experiment proved, we actually improve our performance. This is why so many employment and physical-adventure programmes are designed to push you outside your comfort zone. I use the word 'push' because, as you'll notice, that is precisely what's required. You don't just fall out of your comfort zone unconsciously; it requires effort, which, for a great many of us, is fraught with difficulty. But if we live as though our comfort zones are set in stone, we're placing a limitation on our lives that we'll never go beyond.

Why do we like to be in control?

If asked, most people would rather be in control of a situation than not, right? Why? Well, it's not merely about liking the idea of having personal autonomy or the luxury of choice. In their paper, 'Born to Choose: The Origins and Value of the Need for Control', researchers Leotti, Iyengar and Ochsner concluded that our need for control is most likely a 'biological imperative for survival'.[4] Though it operates at a deeper, subconscious level, being in control of a situation means our survival is more likely. We exercise our control by making choices, and each choice we make reinforces the perception of control and self-efficacy, which, the researchers claim, is essential for an individual's general well-being. When I'm in control of my environment – and my emotions – and I face no threat to my survival, I feel more confident. It makes sense, right?

The learning zone

The 'push' from the comfort zone enables us to enter what theorists refer to as 'the learning zone' or, sometimes, 'the success zone', and it's here that the 'magic' happens. It's the space in which we develop and build on our existing abilities, but it can also be very stressful. Why?

Because out here, there is risk. For the most part, it's emotional or social risk that we're facing, but as we know, our minds and bodies have evolved with a stress response that swings into action if it perceives that we are in any kind of danger (be it physical or emotional). So we feel stress and anxiety as a warning signal. As explained by Dr Aisling Leonard-Curtin,[5] chartered psychologist and co-author of *The Power of Small*, entering the learning zone 'requires a willingness to feel this anxiety', which, as you can imagine, few of us really relish. In the learning zone, we are in uncharted territory with situations beyond our everyday terms of reference. We're unsure if we have the skillset to handle the situation and it feels out of control (which our survival instinct does not like). We're in an unknown situation and because of the perceived fears that surround it, our bodies are doling out the adrenaline to help us cope and ensure our survival. Again this needn't be in the face of legitimate danger, it could be any situation where you are uncomfortable – a social gathering, a meeting, a tricky phone call – any situation that is unfamiliar or unnerving to you, where you don't feel that you are in control.

What's the big deal about the unknown?

Dr Sinead Lynch, counselling psychologist and psychotherapist, explained to me that when we worry about something, such as the 'unknown', the connection from the emotional part of the brain to the cognitive part of the brain is activated.[6] Neurologists have actually found that the connections are stronger in the emotional–cognitive direction. This means that it is natural for our emotions to overtake our good sense, resulting in worry. What's more, when it comes to the 'unknown', there can be three core emotions at play: loneliness, shame and fear. We fear the unknown in case it causes us emotional pain.

'We want to avoid these experiences because they are emotionally painful,' explains Dr Lynch. 'If, for example, going to a party is stepping out of your comfort zone, you might be thinking worrying thoughts like "people won't talk to me". On a deeper level, these thoughts could be coming from feelings of shame (about yourself) or feelings of loneliness or loss (from a previous experience) mixed with the fear of how humiliating it would be if you were left standing alone at a social event. Therefore, the idea of going to a party would naturally stress you out and you would most likely want to retreat to the safety of your comfort zone. It's very important to take our emotions into account because they provide us with key information that we can address compassionately rather than forcing ourselves to break out of our comfort zone without understanding what it is we're fearing.'

For me, the fear of the unknown generally relates back to a lack of control, which, we know, puts our survival instinct on high alert.

So, why would we want to enter the learning zone?

As explained by Dr Aisling Leonard-Curtin: 'If we stay within our comfort zones, we will not make many, or any, changes in our lives.'[7] When you make the jump out of your comfort zone and into the learning zone, eventually the unfamiliar becomes familiar and your anxiety normalises. An example here is when you feel a surge of social anxiety around meeting a new group of people. When the first few minutes of awkward pleasantries are out of the way, your surroundings become familiar and your anxiety reduces from a boil to a simmer. The unknown becomes known. That which first seemed insurmountable or scary or beyond your capabilities has lost its threatening horns. You feel you are regaining control of the situation. This is what's known as a 'stretch-zone' experience. We dip into the learning zone to 'stretch' our comfort zone.

Optimal anxiety

Stretch-zone experiences give rise to something called 'optimal anxiety' – two words that for so long, I would have refused to put together. Remember the Yerkes and Dodson experiment? When the mice were put under a little bit of stress, their performance improved. This is optimal anxiety at work. It's when we experience slightly above-average levels of stress or anxiety for a limited time, exposing ourselves to it and allowing it to settle, before the anxiety is then neutralised. With optimal anxiety, we are managing the situation and making a choice to be *in* the situation, which instils a sense of control.

As explained by Dr Aisling Leonard-Curtin: 'The secret here is to break far enough outside of our comfort zones so that we experience some optimal anxiety – this is actually a good sign. In this optimal-anxiety zone, we are motivated to drive towards a richer, fuller, more meaningful life. This kind of anxiety is really important from an evolutionary perspective to motivate you to take action and to give your brain a signal that you are in fact doing something novel, something that has a higher risk, but with the potential of greater rewards. As such, with this level of optimal anxiety, you are more mindful and pay more attention in the moment to the task at hand, enhancing your overall skills and attention to detail.'

The time limit

Understanding that we only stretch our comfort zones for a limited time is crucial. 'You need to be careful not to overextend your comfort zone too much in any given moment so that you remain firmly planted within your self-care zone,' explains Dr Leonard-Curtin. 'Your self-care zone is that zone in which you experience some uncomfortable anxiety; however, this anxiety is communicating that you are doing something that matters to you. When you break so far outside your comfort zone, however, that you are also outside of your self-care zone, this is when you are in dangerous territory.'[8]

The jump from the comfort zone to the learning zone is what we're striving for because it's where we grow. That said, because it's a jump that takes us from anxiety-neutral to anxiety (where we experience fear, uncertainty and uneasiness), it requires caution. There is a limit on the amount of stress or anxiety we can experience before it goes from optimal to bad. It seems there's only so long we can experience a lack of control before we want to rein it back in. To go back to Yerkes and Dodson, when their mice experienced too much stress, their performance went downhill. Go too far in the success zone, and you're in danger of experiencing heightened levels of stress and anxiety on a daily basis that will soon push you over the edge into another state of being: the danger or panic zone.

Dr Shahram Heshmat, Associate Professor at the University of Illinois and author of *Science of Choice*, stated: 'When levels of arousal are too low (boredom) and when levels of arousal are too high (anxiety or fear) performance is likely to suffer. Worrying about how you will perform on a test may actually contribute to a lower test score. Under situations of low arousal, the mind is unfocused. In contrast, under situations of high stimulation, the focus of attention is too narrow, and important information may be lost. The optimal situation is moderate arousal.'[9]

Another term for moderate arousal? Optimal anxiety.

The panic zone

Spend too long in the learning zone and you'll begin to see signs of physical and emotional burnout, which will bring you closer and closer to the panic zone. This, as you'll know from the times when you've simply pushed yourself too far or endured too much stress for an extended period of time, will have more negative effects on your well-being than positive.

People who spend all of their time in the success zone, where high levels of stress are a daily inevitability, tend to be unhealthy. They deplete their mental and physical reserves that are there to help them succeed in the first place. This is something I know all too well. My crippling anxiety first hit me when I kept pushing myself in a job that I didn't like, getting more and more stressed out and physically unwell as I tried to ignore what felt right in search of what I had previously defined as 'success'. Without even realising it, I was living in the panic zone, and it was quite some time before I found my way back to any feeling of comfort.

If you work a seventy-hour week, chained to a desk, you might be familiar with this. Nobody really wants to be here but it can happen easily if you allow yourself to go too far. Though it was once seen as a badge of honour to work yourself into oblivion, no learning can happen here. You're not going to be productive and you're probably not in control. And that's without going into the negative side effects of how stress can affect your sleep – a lack of which can further impact your performance and your mental health. In this state, your mind and body are too busy dealing with anxiety and trying to keep your head above water, to handle the task at hand.

As explained by Dr Aisling Leonard-Curtin: 'In my experience, working with people as a psychologist, when people go into this danger or panic zone, it can be completely overwhelming and counterproductive. Rather than helping the person live a richer, fuller life, they have such a horrible, and sometimes trauma-tising, experience that they retreat right back into their comfort zone once more and are actually less likely to engage in further actions outside their comfort zone.'[10]

Today, I might veer towards the unhelpful side of the success zone if I constantly put myself in situations that make me uneasy without taking some downtime in between to come back to centre, to return to my comfort zone. Unfortunately, when we allow ourselves to get to the point of burnout, without recognising the warning signs along the way, our boundaries can actually shrink, leading us right back to square one, cocooned by a limiting and seemingly rigid comfort zone, fearful of ever stepping foot outside of it again. I say this from experience.

The, erm, sh*t zone

There is another zone that's often left out of these model descriptions and that's 'the sh*t zone'. (And, no, I won't hold my breath for a Nobel Prize for the coining of that term.) This place sits well below the comfort zone; it's the place where we suffer and languish. Here, we are merely trying to survive. On a graph, it's not a stress peak, but a trough. We might be physically unwell or emotionally depleted or both – we are definitely not comfortable. This is where I found myself back then, after wandering blindly into the panic zone by pushing myself into a job that I didn't want and resisting the stress that my body was using as a messenger to tell me to hightail it right out of there. By the time I got to the sh*t zone, I was merely trying to get through the day. My long journey back towards some semblance of a comfort zone – which at that stage, had become more limited than ever – is chronicled in greater detail in *Owning It* (*cough* shameless plug).

The sh*t zone checklist

It's hard to miss it if you've crossed over into the sh*t zone – it's about as subtle as a bull in a china shop – but here are a few of its nasty red flags to look out for:

- complete inability to make decisions
- feeling totally overwhelmed about everything
- feeling that you are not in control of your environment
- trouble sleeping
- heightened anxiety
- series of panic attacks
- basic tasks are a challenge
- tears, lots of tears
- general inability to cope

The loop

From my personal experience – and please remember, most of what you read here is just my take on things – these states of being are not necessarily linear or stacked on top of one another, with the sh*t zone right at the bottom and the panic zone right at the top. For me, they're interlinked on a loop.

Roll with me for a moment.

We spend most of our time in the comfort zone. We muster the courage to enter the learning zone and, here, we make a choice: take it slowly, learning and developing and eventually creating a new comfort zone; or keep pushing ourselves into the upper echelons of the learning zone. If we go too far here, we wind up in the panic zone – think of Icarus flying too close to the sun.

This is precisely what happened to me, and why I found myself down in the doldrums of the sh*t zone, having to start all over again. I had come full circle, so to speak.

It's worth being mindful that you can easily go from the learning zone to the panic zone and from there, you can quickly find yourself in the sh*t zone, which is why you need to be awake and aware of that likelihood. To go from the comfort zone to the learning zone is the only jump that requires conscious work.

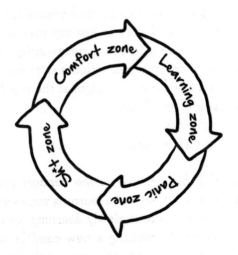

The ideal

So with an awareness of each of the states of being, here is what I consider the ideal scenario for a life of fulfilment that's neither too stressful nor too dull.

For starters, we do not and should not want to spend our lives in the learning zone. Don't make this mistake. Instead, we want to lean into it, expanding our comfort zone, slowly but surely. Understanding that your comfort zone is never a set thing is one of the first steps to facing your fears and increasing your confidence over time. Consider the comfort zone as your place of stability but know that it absolutely can stretch and that's the goal. It's your home, and the learning zone is an adventurous foreign destination. You take brief trips to the learning zone to broaden your horizons. By doing so, you expand your comfort zone and that in itself is a success. You have a 'stretch-zone experience' that gives rise to optimal anxiety. The key, though, is that it's incremental as opposed to diving head first off the deep end and then struggling to get back to the surface. By dipping in, you retain a sense of control, which is necessary for our well-being.

You don't spend too long in the learning zone because if you do, you wear yourself out, potentially landing yourself in the panic zone, experiencing full-blown anxiety where you're too stressed to function and your performance drops off sharply. This happens if you go above optimal anxiety. In this state, your brain starts to produce an overload of stress hormones with which it simply cannot cope. If that happens, you run the risk of shrinking back your comfort zone. Just as it can expand, it can also retract if you consistently push yourself beyond your limits. If this happens, it can serve to reinforce the thinking that challenging yourself is a bad idea. Instead, you should dip in and out of the learning zone, experiencing the sweet spot of optimal anxiety, before returning to your comfort zone, bringing this new experience with you and adding your newfound skills and abilities to your arsenal of tools. You expand your control.

Dr Aisling Leonard-Curtin and her partner, fellow psychologist Dr Trish Leonard-Curtin wrote: 'Maintaining task-focused attention whilst experiencing optimal anxiety is important to how effective you will be at engaging in your chosen activity. If you shift into self-focused attention trying to control or manipulate the anxiety, you are likely to take your attention away from your chosen activity and become fixated on your anxiety. Naturally, this will no longer be helpful for you. The secret is to find your self-care zone outside your comfort zone where optimal anxiety and task-focused attention are most likely. Here, you stand the best chance of making long-term sustainable changes.'[11]

Exercise
(BY DR TRISH LEONARD-CURTIN):

Here is a simple template for stepping outside of your comfort zone (created by Dr Trish Leonard-Curtin). Document your experience in your notebook.

1 *Connect with your values and intention for the action outside your comfort zone, i.e. what makes this important enough that you're willing to feel anxious?*

2 *Given how important you've rated your value, on a scale from 1 to 10, rate the level of anxiety that you are willing to feel when you engage in this action.*

3 *Commit to engaging in the action, connecting as fully as possible to your five senses when doing it.*

4 *If your anxiety level goes above the level you decided in advance, take some time to reconnect with your five senses and assess the impact of this on your anxiety.*

5 *At the end of the activity, assess whether you were within your optimal-anxiety range for the majority of the time. If so, you can go a little further outside your comfort zone next time. If not, it's best to do something smaller next time and build your way up to the original activity.*

Many people I meet – and for so long in my own experience – say their energy is focused on trying not to feel the anxiety or fear or uneasiness that goes along with stepping outside of their comfort zone. But remember, this is not the goal. That kind of anxiety isn't going anywhere and trying to avoid it is only going to make you feel worse, or you'll wind up berating yourself if you go into a situation hoping to feel as cool as a cucumber before realising that that's just not possible. We are not trying to 'conquer' all feelings of fear and live our lives as some unearthly, powerful being (but if you've cracked that secret, do let me know). Instead, we're going to manage it and strategise and learn to work *with* the fear of failure which, in itself, will begin the process of instilling confidence. And don't forget, those feelings of fear actually benefit you in situations of optimal anxiety. Without them, you might not succeed or do as well as you'd hoped.

So while fear shouldn't hold us back, we don't necessarily want to get rid of it. We all feel fear and most of us have doubted ourselves to the point of quitting or hoping that the ground would open up and swallow us in a new and unnerving experience, but when we persevere in spite of this, it makes the eventual success all the sweeter.

What separates those who achieve success (again, everyone's idea of success is different) from those who prefer to maintain the status quo is how they process their feelings of fear. What they do. What they decide. How they interpret their anxiety. Don't doubt that almost every one of us will still come out the other side saying 'phew', breathing an enormous sigh of relief and being glad it's over. And don't forget that the act of making a choice – even if it's a choice that scares you – is still an act of being in control.

We all inhabit a comfort zone but its size and characteristics vary. Is yours small and rigid? Big and flexible? Open to negotiation? That's up to you.

The importance of being realistic

Time and time again, we hear the phrase: 'Do something every day that scares you.' For most of us, this is unrealistic and unhealthy. You can't go from one terrifying experience to another and on to the next thing all in the same direction without taking time in between to process the benefits and go back to that anxiety-neutral base. Well, you can if you want to, but it *will* wear you down. Instead, embrace the more realistic perspective of minor incremental changes which, over time, enable major improvements.

Small slow steps –> Big improvements

Small changes accumulate and each one builds on the previous one, all the time building your confidence. Expanding your comfort zone is a long-term project. It's too overwhelming to go from A to Z without a breather in between. It's also worth remembering that not all challenges you face or set yourself need to be one bigger than the last, growing exponentially in terms of fear. So instead of deciding that one day you'll give a speech in front of ten people, the next day 100, the next day 10,000, go for ten, then give yourself time to process and appreciate the jump you've made. Don't get the promotion you've long been dreaming of and then say, 'Well, I want more now', and push yourself over the edge. Yes, it's good to have drive, but sometimes you need to let yourself enjoy the comfort too. Remember, you're aiming for optimal anxiety and no further. What's more, if you leapfrog from one to the next to the *next* in quick succession, not only do you risk overdoing it, you diminish the significance of your initial bravery.

It's important to realise that you can take steps outside your comfort zone in different directions too. Climbing the mountain vertically isn't the only option; you can zig-zag up it. Take it slowly with one thing before nudging your comfort zone in another direction, such as trying a food you've always said you wouldn't like or meditating for ten minutes (which is something some people find unnerving) or taking a class in something that interests you. Expanding your comfort zone doesn't always have to involve petrifying experiences, there's plenty of room for small boundary stretches that are no less significant to the overall picture of building confidence.

It's not all bad

You're probably thinking here that the poor old comfort zone gets a lot of bad press. We blame it for holding us back. We demonise it as the roadblock standing between us and success. But as far as I'm concerned, it's very important that we return to our comfort zone, that we respect it and that we embrace it. Otherwise, we would be constantly stressed out and unhealthy. There's got to be room for learning and for comfort in our lives. The comfort zone is our equilibrium, where we rest and assess and take stock and find our feet.

All going well, the boundaries of your comfort zone will open up, enabling personal development, increased confidence and the breaking down of preconceived fear.

What Is Fear?

THIS CHAPTER is a necessary primer on the ways in which our mind processes fear. Unfortunately, a certain amount of jargon is inescapable when discussing the human brain, so you'll have to bear with me. However, I find it incredibly empowering to delve beyond the surface and really wrap my head around not just the what, but the how and the why. This is a more holistic understanding of fear that, I believe, will better enable us to manage it in the long run. So, jump back to this chapter if you need a reminder of how the amygdala works, and what the other *Lord-of-the-Rings*-sounding terminology is all about.

What is fear?

Practically speaking, fear is a physical response to an observable danger. It's generated in the mind by a specific stimulus, such as seeing a tarantula crawling up a wall in your home (unless you're of the minority who has a particular fondness for hairy, eight-legged creatures) or being chased by a predator in the wild. Fear happens the moment we sense a threat to our survival. It acts immediately. Fear's primary role is to keep us alive.

Though it can be hard to articulate, we all know what this fear feels like. It helps us focus and deal with a threat as best we can in real time. For the most part, it feels like our insides – our hearts, our tummies, our everything – would rather be outsides. Symptoms of fear arise as a result of the release of hormones (namely adrenaline and cortisol, the latter of which is slow-releasing) triggered by our brain when it senses danger, be it tangible and realistic (e.g. a shark swimming right for us with a glint in his eye and his mouth open) or perceived (e.g. swimming in shark-free waters and fearing that one might be there).

We start to sweat, we tremble, our hearts race, our pupils dilate, we feel like running away, our mouths dry up, we struggle to breathe, our blood pressure rises and our digestive system shuts down. In short, we can refer to these physical reactions as a 'stress response' or the 'fight-or-flight response', which you've probably heard of. While we know that our stress response is very necessary in certain situations (i.e. situations where we need it to keep us alive), the way we're experiencing it in modern-day life is often unnecessary.

A lot of the time, it's a false alarm and very inconvenient. For example, my brain perceiving that if I go on live television, I might actually die or that if I go to India I will spend two weeks in bed with Delhi Belly. But that's the thing to remember about fear: it engages in your mind and body regardless of whether the threat is observable and right in front of you or something you think could happen. As far as your brain circuitry is concerned, the fact that your fear might be perceived doesn't matter; when danger is sensed, it sends in the troops. Think about it: there is rarely a genuine threat to our survival in the twenty-first century (as there would have been back in hunter-gatherer times), yet our brain still responds in the same damn way. It evolved to protect us, such as instinctively feeling fearful if we were about to fall off the side of a cliff and die, but today it's protective impulse can actually hinder us, such as feeling fear when we arrive at a party full of people we don't know – and that, in turn, hinders our potential for self-confidence. Our hearts start to race so we can run or fight but, on most occasions, there is nothing to run away from and nothing to fight. Without a legitimate threat, the hormones bounce around our bodies with nowhere to go, leaving us feeling as though we're about to be chopped up when no such thing will occur. It's exhausting. And too much of it, too often, throws our careful balance of hormones out of whack. The thing is, while we've evolved enormously since hunter-gatherer times, the part of our brain that processes fear has not.

It's still evolving and we've got a long way to go before this not-so-useful kink is ironed out.

Perceived fear

It's because of the life-saving nature of fear that total fearlessness is never the goal. We just wouldn't survive for too long if we lived without fear. Fear protects us when danger is tangible and realistic. It's our *perceived* fears that we need to work on.

Perceived fear or anxiety is the feeling of being at risk when there is no imminent or observable danger. It's a psychological response to the *idea* of potential danger. Typically, it's more future-oriented, such as the Sunday fear, when you dread what Monday morning will bring.

Dr Shahram Heshmat told me it also tends to be more self-focused. He describes it as 'objectless apprehension' and 'nameless dread'. Perceived fears can hold us back, such as the fear of failure, whereas immediate fears, such as hungry tigers, keep us alive.[12]

Interestingly, of all the emotions we can experience, our brains devote the most space and energy to fear. As we hone in on how our brain works in relation to fear, bear in mind that this kind of research is happening right now; the mystery of the brain is still being unravelled so by the time you're reading this, there may well have been more discoveries.

The limbic system

The limbic system can be thought of as a wide network of structures each of which serves its own function. The limbic system and all that it houses, including the amygdala, the hypothalamus and the hippocampus, is often considered to be the feeling and reacting brain. Your emotional life happens here. It's the primordial brain network underpinning your mood (so feel free to blame it the next time someone asks you what the hell is wrong with you). What's more, the job of this network is to ensure not just your survival on a day-to-day basis but the survival of the human race as well – no pressure.

The amygdala

Based on what we know so far, the part of the brain that is most relevant when it comes to fear is the amygdala (pronounced 'ah-mig-da-lah'). The amygdala is an almond-shaped structure of neurons located behind each ear (as is the case with all brain structures, we have two of them) and it plays a significant role in our emotions, emotional behaviour and motivation. This is where our body's alarm circuit lies. According to NYU neuroscientist Joseph LeDoux (who is considered to be the leading expert on how our brain processes fear), when the amygdala is negatively stimulated (i.e. when a window of your home is broken), the alarm goes off and we experience a state of fear.

The amygdala is the limbic system's star player; it receives sensory information about the external world from another part of the brain called the thalamus, at which point it reacts automatically. It does this before your mind even knows what the potential danger is. It kicks into gear based on perception, before the facts of the situation are established. If it gets a message that there is danger in the environment, it will send out its own messages to the parts of the brain involved with emotional reactivity, such as the adrenal cortex, where our stress hormones emanate from, to perhaps freeze, run and increase your heart rate, to do whatever is necessary to get you to safety. And all of this happens automatically.

It's quite hard to distinguish between fear caused by an observable danger and fear that we perceive (anxiety). They both contain the idea of danger or dread and they affect the body in very similar ways (though anxiety is longer lasting). However, there is one notable difference. As explained by Emory University Behavioural Neuro-scientist Michael Davis, fear and anxiety emanate from different parts of the amygdala. The fear response, he says, comes from the region responsible for commands of bodily responses associated with fear (and remember, fear is all about that physical reaction to get you to safety). On the other hand, anxiety is said to originate in another area of the amygdala responsible for emotions that mediates slower onset, longer-lasting behavioural responses that can continue long after a perceived threat has gone. When it comes to a lack of confidence and a fear of failure, this behavioural response is what we're exploring.[13]

Stress

Though it's an essential part of our brain, sh*t gets real when the amygdala over-performs (mine just won't quit). I've always described it as a particularly cautious parent going to great lengths to protect their child from potential danger, when their child is already swaddled in cotton wool and living in Fort Knox. The amygdala can be triggered often and unnecessarily when we experience too much stress.

Different again to fear or anxiety, stress is another term worth clarifying. Clinical psychologist Dr Ian Gargan has it sussed: 'I would always say stress is when your internal resources are overwhelmed by the environmental needs. Effectively, you perceive that you don't have the resources in you to be able to take care of, or become in control of, what's going on in your environment.'[14]

We don't specifically have to feel afraid but, when experienced often, stress can wear down the higher-thinking, more rational part of our brains, leaving the amygdala in charge without an adult to steer it in the right direction. If this happens, the amygdala is more likely to mistakenly identify threats, sending out fear responses that are meant to protect us, but that just make us feel as though we've been strapped to a train track. This – and I am speaking here from my own experience – is how chronic stress can lead to anxiety and why someone might suffer a panic attack when there's nothing obvious to be panicked about. (I remember one of my worst ones erupting like a volcano inside me as I was sitting on the couch in the comfort of my own home; you'd never expect it to happen in this scenario.)

Fear conditioning and the hippocampus

But wait, there's more (bear with me). The amygdala also works a lot on fear association, which, in scientific circles, has been called 'fear conditioning' or 'fear learning'. What might come as a surprise to know is that we are born with only two fears: the fear of falling and the fear of loud noises – not spiders, not aeroplanes, not scary movies and certainly not the fear of Mondays. Absolutely everything else that we fear is learned or 'conditioned'.

To understand fear conditioning, it helps to first under-stand classical conditioning.

Classical conditioning was noted in the 1920s by Ivan Pavlov (unfortunately, no Pavlova dessert was involved).[15]

Pavlov's experiment involved ringing a bell and giving his dog some treats. It was known that all dogs salivate automatically when they are given food. This happens from the moment a puppy is born because the puppy needs food to survive. It's instinctive. What Pavlov noticed, however, was that when he introduced a stimulus, such as the sound of a bell as the dog was given his food, a learned association was made for the dog. After several bell-ringing feeding sessions, all that was needed was the sound of the bell – and not the sight or smell of the food – to cause the dog to salivate. It had the same physiological reaction even though there was no treat involved (bit sh*t for the dog). In short, the dog's brain had been conditioned by a memory to bring about the same behavioural response when triggered by a neutral stimulus.

Now, back to fear conditioning.

Fear conditioning is a form of classical conditioning whereby we associate a sh*tty, fearful experience with a neutral context or stimulus, such as a room or a sound or even a person. With fear conditioning, Pavlov's theory still applies, but instead of a positive reaction, it's obviously quite negative. In terms of the brain, fear conditioning involves communication between the amygdala and another part of the brain, also said to live within the limbic system: the hippocampus.

The hippocampus

The hippocampus is hugely important when it comes to perceived fear – in fact, it's just as relevant as the amygdala. It is considered to be the brain's primary memory centre and it's essential when it comes to recognising previously experienced, or similar, events.

In terms of fear, the hippocampus provides contextual information (e.g. the circumstances surrounding a memory or an association) direct to the amygdala, to help inform its response to the perceived danger. What's more, the hippocampus doesn't just recall the black-and-white facts of the memory to the amygdala, it forms representations of events with emotional significance. The amygdala and the hippocampus work together in both directions; it's a two-way street. The amygdala influences the fear memories that are stored in the hippocampus – as an experience occurs – and then the hippocampus will relay that same memory (and the associated emotions) if something similar occurs in the future.

With fear conditioning, an association can be forged by the brain a lot more quickly than would have been the case for Pavlov's dog. Pavlov needed to repeat the bell-food scenario a few times for the dog to salivate, but sometimes it takes just one bad experience to bring about a fearful association that will affect your confidence when faced with similar situations in the future. What's more, the specific memory that first triggered the feelings of fear in your body is more securely lodged in your brain's memory system (the hippocampus). So it's a more powerful and longer-lasting memory. Unfortunately, this means it's that bit harder to crack.

Think back to your childhood. It's very likely that you can vividly remember one fearful experience you had as a child, whereas you might struggle to recall details of a more positive experience that happened at a similar age.

The most famous (and on a side note, incredibly cruel) example of human fear conditioning is the case of Little Albert, an eleven-month-old-baby used as the subject in John Watson and Rosalie Rayner's study back in 1920.[16] Like all babies, Albert had a natural fear of extremely loud noises but he had no aversion to, say, a white rat. Nobody is born with this fear. So Watson and Rayner presented him with a white rat, and when he reached to touch it, they struck a hammer against a steel bar just behind his head (and yes, you should be wincing as you read this). After seeing the rat and hearing the frightening noise, Albert would then burst into tears at the mere sight of the rat. What's more, the baby would cry at the sight of objects that resembled the white rat, such as a white dog or a white coat.

An example in your own life (that wasn't forced upon you by unethical scientists) might be if you fell into water as a child and still grapple with a fear of being out of your depth. This was my experience. I was three years old, standing at the edge of a swimming pool, wrapped in a towel with my arms inside it and I slipped on a wet tile and fell in. Twenty-seven years later, I can still see the bubbles in the water as I realised what was happening. Needless to say, addressing my confidence surrounding water-related activities is on my list.

Though the same threat might not be there today, your brain recognises a similar scenario and instantly recalls your fearful experience. Annoyingly, it produces the same fear response that it did back then in order to ensure the experience doesn't happen now. If you have experienced something similar in the past – such as a panic attack in a particular restaurant or an uncomfortable experience speaking up in class – then you have heightened anxiety to the present situation. You start to feel panicky if you return to the same restaurant even though the restaurant had nothing to do with it. You can consider this the scene-of-the-crime syndrome. Your brain is designed to make these sharp associations to keep you from harm. Necessary as it can be on occasion, this is, again, another function of the brain that can negatively impact on our lives and hold us back.

When my anxiety was at its absolute worst in 2014, I went away for a few days with my parents to their house in the countryside. The aim was to help me relax and ensure I had constant company because I was feeling so low and my partner was away with work. I loved the house and the part of the country it was in, and I'd had lots of happy experiences there, so, surely, being there would help. However, because my anxiety was so bad, and I had some severe panic attacks when I was there, a link was formed in my mind – though I didn't realise it at the time – between excruciating anxiety and that house, which was a neutral, innocent context.

I went back home, and did what I had to do to deal with my anxiety. A few months later, I went back to the house in the countryside. And though I was no longer struggling with anxiety to the same extent, the minute I was back inside those four walls, the memories of my previous experience came flooding back to me and I began to feel the physical effects of anxiety as though no time had passed and no progress had been made. I found it so hard to be there (as well as feeling pretty stupid about the whole thing). It felt like an elephant had taken up permanent residency on my chest and no amount of rationalising that the house couldn't be causing me anxiety helped. Neither would countless cups of tea. I had been conditioned – with just one trip – to associate a fearful experience with a neutral context. How was I going to tackle this one?

It's worth noting that not every fear or aversion we have is brought about by a traumatic experience. We also pick up on cues from those around us as we are developing, especially our parents, and what society deems as 'fearful'. So while I was never forced to get in a cage with a boa constrictor, I'd still run faster than Usain Bolt if I knew one was within a fifty-mile radius of me.

Fear extinction

Just as fear conditioning can hinder confidence, fear extinction can rectify things. Fear extinction is the generally accepted theory that a conditioned or learned fear can be greatly reduced, if not extinguished entirely, by repeatedly exposing yourself to the fear-inducing context or stimulus, and realising that there is no real danger.

In scientific terms, it involves creating a conditioned response to counteract the conditioned fear response.

Let us go back to the idea of the restaurant in which we've had a panic attack. If you return to this place – a neutral context – one time after the attack, you'll likely produce a stress response. If, however, you repeatedly expose yourself to the same restaurant and have new experiences there, your fear response will run out of steam and the association will eventually break.

A more recent experiment was that of scientist Mark Barad in UCLA, involving rats (poor rodents, they get a pretty sh*t time of it), a certain sound and an electric shock. After experiencing the shock, the rats learned to brace themselves upon hearing the sound. Fear extinction works in the opposite way to fear conditioning. When the rats were then exposed to the sound several times without being shocked, their fear response actually declined – their association of the sound with pain lessened over time, until they reached a point where the sound elicited no fear response whatsoever. They no longer feared it. Scientists have theorised that while fear-related memories live in the amygdala, fear extinction memories are transferred from the amygdala to the prefrontal cortex (PFC) which – and we'll get to this – is where logic and reason happens. Now, the new memory that lives in the PFC will override the fear response from the amygdala about the same context or stimulus.

Though it wasn't easy, this was what eventually got me over my own fear-conditioned response to my parents' house in the countryside. I had to go back again and face it but this time I expected to feel afraid, and I wasn't shocked by it. I had to endure it in the short term to overcome my fear in the long term – and it felt really crap at first, don't get me wrong. I exposed myself to the situation for a longer period of time, so that the anxiety in my body could eventually settle. At that point, I was able to create new and more positive associations that eventually calmed my mind, which at last accepted that I wasn't in danger and there was no need to feel panicked there and that what had happened to me that first time was not because of the place, but because of the time in my life and what I was going through. To this day, I still expect these memories to creep in on me when I go to this house, so it doesn't shock me if I feel a bit unsettled at first, but by now, by proactively facing that which brought about a fear response in me, it's pretty much extinguished.

The negativity bias

We've already discussed the way in which a fearful association can lodge in the brain much more quickly and more long term than a positive association. The reason for this is the negativity bias. As countless research papers have shown, we instinctively place a lot more emphasis on the negative than the positive (it's not a case of having a pessimistic outlook on life) and, yet again, we've evolved with this imbalance in order to survive. We react a lot more quickly and more strongly to negative experiences than we do to positive ones. In fact, we place three times as much importance on one negative as we do one positive. Why? Because back in the day, when an enormous amount of the human brain circuitry was developing, we had to react quickly to danger – or anything that appeared to be negative – otherwise we'd run the risk of being gulped down by something higher up the food chain in one fell swoop. We didn't have to respond as strongly or as quickly to positive stimuli because a positive experience was not a matter of life or death. So, give yourself a break for jumping to the worst-case scenario, your brain is just doing overtime on lookout duty.[17]

The prefrontal cortex

From reading this chapter so far, it might sound like we're pretty much f*cked when it comes to fear. The good news, however, is that we all have a little something called the prefrontal cortex (PFC). The amygdala also gets messages from here, which is the higher-thinking part of the brain that is responsible for the most sophisticated aspects of cognition. It's also thought to be one of the newer parts of the brain. When the limbic system is reacting and feeling, the PFC is thinking. For the most part, we want the PFC to be in charge. It's the adult in the situation. All going well, the PFC should moderate a fear response from the amygdala if there's no actual threat to be concerned about, but if we're burning the candles at both ends or consistently stressed out, it doesn't always succeed. The amygdala wins the battle and hijacks the rational part of the brain. Because of this, taking rest and timeouts, and time spent in the comfort zone, is key.

The communication between the PFC and the amygdala happens a little more slowly than the messages that come direct from the thalamus (the part of the brain that gives information to the amygdala). The PFC has to talk to the thalamus first, which then passes on the message to the amygdala. By the time the PFC steps in, the brain has a better sense of what's actually happening. It has awareness. The PFC is involved in the final stages of how we process fear. If there is no threat, the PFC should have the where-withal to calm the amygdala and we should resume our normal state of being. You'll recognise this when you recover from a fright (for example, when the killer in the movie isn't quite dead yet). If there is a genuine threat, it will green light the amygdala's automatic fear response.

The thing is, our brains only realise something is not life-threatening *after* the PFC has assessed the situation, so you can imagine the importance of the PFC when it comes to living a less fearful life. While the amygdala may be the somewhat archaic limbic system's star player, the PFC is yours. And when it comes to perceived fears that stand in the way of your self-confidence, we can use this to our advantage.

So, it's not all doom and gloom in our quest for confidence. This is where the toolkit in Part Two comes in. By road-testing the ways in which we can increase our confidence, we challenge our fears and better understand them, all of which helps to kick our PFC's arse in gear.

Why Do We Fear Failure?

NOW THAT WE have a general understanding of fear and how it works in our minds and bodies, we can move on to one perceived fear in particular: the fear of failure. This is a fear that really affects our day-to-day lives, putting a major spanner in the works of our confidence-building. But what exactly is this kind of fear and where does it come from?

As explained by Dr Aisling Leonard-Curtin, 'the fear of failure is rooted in a fear of not achieving some benchmark that either we've set for ourselves or that someone else has set for us.'

We experience the fear of failure when we have doubts about our ability to succeed in whatever we're taking on. This doubt is common. In cases where it becomes particularly extreme, it can be referred to as atychiphobia, but I fear (ironically) that if we place such definitive labels on ourselves, we'll take them as a given – a fixed thing about us that we cannot change, when we absolutely can.

The fear of failure is hard to define and is probably best understood by examples. Mary has an incredible singing voice but she won't take a chance on a singing career when an opportunity presents itself because she believes she will fail. She perceives that it won't work out, so she doesn't take action. Not only is she afraid of failing, she's afraid of the emotions associated with failing: disappointment, sadness, frustration, the feeling of not being good enough – the list goes on. If she doesn't take action, she can tell herself that it *could* happen; but, if she goes for it, there's a chance it won't happen – and if it doesn't, she will perceive it as a failure.

One of my own? Well, there have been countless, but let's start with the fear of failure I'm experiencing in writing this very book. To be brief – I could talk about this fear all day long – I'm afraid that I won't get it done on time or done to a high enough standard. I'm afraid it will be a critical and commercial flop. I'm afraid it will make me question my ability as a writer. I'm afraid of what all of you will think of me. Now, had I not signed a contract, which means I'm legally obliged to follow through, I might run a million miles away, allowing my behavioural response to this kind of fear to take its course. But the fear of failure that both Mary and I are experiencing is not based on any facts. It's perceived. It's a subconscious belief that we will not succeed that brings about a behavioural response which instinctively wants to hold us back. It's a fear that makes us want to say no and attend only to the tasks in which we're certain we can't fail, the tasks that we can do easily within the boundaries of our comfort zone.

When we fear failure, we are afraid to take action. It's easier not to take action, because if we don't, we can't fail – or so we think. The fear of failure, you may have noticed, can be pretty paralysing.

Where does this particular fear stem from? For starters, it may go back to the old hunter-gatherer times when avoiding failure quite literally meant avoiding death, such as successfully defending yourself against a predator. Today, however, the kinds of scenarios we find ourselves in, such as giving a presentation in work or asking somebody out on a date, are not life or death (though they can sometimes feel like it). But remember: your mind responds to fear the same way today as it did back then, even when it's merely perceived.

As explained by Mind Tools, an online well-being resource, having critical or unsupportive parents can be a cause of the fear of failure for many, because they were routinely undermined or humiliated in childhood and carry those negative feelings into adulthood.

What's more, they suggest that experiencing a traumatic event at some point in early life can also be a cause. 'For example, say that, several years ago, you gave an important presentation in front of a large group and you did very poorly. The experience might have been so terrible that you became afraid of failing in other things. And you carry that fear even now, years later.'[18]

There are two other reasons why I think so many of us are struggling with the fear of failure. The first takes us back again to good old evolution.

For a very long time, humans were not at the top of the food chain. I think it was mostly lions that ruled the roost, but I'm no David Attenborough and I'm getting that info from *The Lion King*, a scientifically reputable source, you'll agree. In my opinion, all of the fears we've talked about thus far could easily be correlated with where we ranked on the food chain then and now. It might seem tenuous but think about it: until very recently, we found ourselves smack bang in the middle of the food chain. According to Yuval Noah Harari (author of *Sapiens: A Brief History of Humankind* and TED-talking legend),[19] back then we hunted smaller creatures within our means, all the while being hunted ourselves by larger predators. This was the way of the world for millions of years and though we can't imagine a scenario in which we're not in charge, it was only in the last 100,000 years that we jumped to the top of the food chain and dominated the world. This is a blip of time in the grand scheme of things. It was a hasty and premature jump in terms of evolution and, physically, it should never have been possible. Were we ever going to grow larger and stronger than lions? I don't think so. But our bigger brains, with the advantage of our prefrontal cortex, meant we were able to outsmart larger predators by domesticating fire and making tools that enabled us to hunt far beyond what our bodies' strength would have been capable of, which eventually led to a cognitive revolution - an agricultural revolution and an industrial revolution - and right up to where we find ourselves today (and yes, that's a whistle-stop tour of the history of humankind - I definitely recommend reading *Sapiens* for a more detailed account of human evolution).

Mentally, we were stronger but physically we were not, and this, I believe, has a lot to do with our collective experience of fear that we still carry around today. When you think about a lion on land or a shark in the sea - you see them as unequivocally confident, right? They're strolling or swimming around, not a care in the world, deciding if they want to eat à la carte or just get takeout tonight. They're not thinking about potential threats or ways in which things might go tits-up for them. This, according to Harari, is because their rise to the top of the food chain happened slowly over millions of years and this has given them an inherent confidence.

They built on it over time. They certainly don't doubt themselves in the same way we do.

For us humans, our rise to the top happened so quickly that we didn't have the time necessary to ease into our new role. We leapfrogged from intern to CEO without working our way up the ranks. We didn't have the experience and this left us with insecurities about being right for the job. In his book, Harari outlines that nature's most powerful predators have spent millions of years at the top of the heap; centuries of dominion have filled them with self-confidence. Meanwhile, sapiens (that's us) have been considered 'underdogs of the Savannah' until very recently, so to Harari, and me, it makes sense that we would be anxious about our newfound position. While this isn't anything you'll be aware of in your own contemporary experience, the fact that we've risen to the top so quickly (socially, not genetically or physically) is a likely marker for why we're collectively filled with self-doubt. It should have taken us millions of years to get to where we are, by which point we might not experience any fears whatsoever. Maybe that will still happen, but we sure as hell won't be around to see it. In terms of humans versus larger predators today, while we might win an argument with an ape because of our superior cognitive abilities, they could still, without much effort at all, rip our bloody heads off, and what good would our hyperbolic vocabulary be to us then?

Another reason I think the fear of failure is something so commonly grappled with goes back to our childhoods. Again, this is nothing scientifically concrete, but for me it explains a lot. Think back to your formative years for a moment: by and large, we are all taught to do our best, to be safe, not to take risks, to colour inside the lines, to do our homework, not to get into trouble, to toe the party line and, ultimately, not to fail. Taking risks was not encouraged, which was partly for our own safety (e.g. you should never cross the road until the green man appears) and partly so that we had the best chance in life (e.g. not failing your exams). Failure in school meant being held back or not getting where we needed - or, perhaps, where we were expected - to be. It had nothing but negative connotations. It meant a big red F on your paper. This may seem like a generalisation, but from childhood right through to early adulthood, we are largely conditioned by parents and teachers to avoid failure. We're conditioned instead to strive for success, which, I believe, makes us uncomfortable with the concept of failure as we grow up.

It's no bad thing, and our teachers certainly meant well, but the residual aversion to failure can throw up problems in adulthood where some amount of failure is inevitable - especially if you dream big.

Now, think about most working environments today where those who rise to the top of the ranks are considered risk-takers and game-changers; they're the kind of people who absolutely go outside the lines or the box and break the rules. As adults, this kind of behaviour is actually rewarded, but it's quite a leap from childhood when risk was avoided at all costs (and where this kind of person would have been considered a troublemaker, and their behaviour frowned upon, in a school environment). There is a clear discrepancy here. But what changes in that time? When are we supposed to make the flip from play-it-safer to rule-breaker? For a good many of us, we don't, and we continue into adulthood and our working lives as people who don't dive in and learn from their mistakes, as people who follow the rules and get in line. We've been doing it all our lives and so it's quite natural to dislike the idea of getting it wrong.

As a kid, I was the ultimate good girl and high achiever. I never once got detention in school. I almost never failed to turn in my homework and if, for some reason, I didn't get to it, I'd always have a legitimate excuse and I'd be in a blind panic to get to the teacher and explain my situation before he or she scolded me in front of the class. I dotted my is and crossed my ts and did what I was told. Meanwhile, some of the others seemed to breeze in and out of class without a care in the world. If they got in trouble, it didn't upset them. If they failed a test, they weren't fussed. Whatever I did, I put my mind to it and worked hard and prepared to such an extent that I'd never fail. Granted, I wasn't a straight A student but, in eighteen years of education, I never flunked one exam.

You're probably assuming that my parents were a pair of hard asses who piled on the pressure and that would be a likely explanation for my goodie-two-shoes formative years – however, they were anything but. Maybe that's because I did well on my own initiative and so they didn't have to. They were always supportive and all-you-can-do-is-do-your-best believers. I'm not sure of the exact source of my fear of putting a foot wrong, but I do have an older brother who is freakishly smart (he was the kind of kid who excelled in English and Art but also in Maths, where most kids would do well in either creative subjects or scientific subjects but rarely both – the bastard). Perhaps, subconsciously, he set the bar for me. Where a lot of it came naturally to him, it was that bit harder for me (this is not a poor-me story) and with him paving the way, I wanted to do as well as I could. This was the model that I followed. You might say I was just a good student but it was more so a fear of failure that motivated me.

And that was in the 1990s, before the advent of social media, when few outside of my family would have been aware of my successes and failures. Then, it was about what your parents or your teacher thought of your efforts; now it's what the whole world thinks. Though there's plenty of it, you don't need quantitative research to know that anxiety, and the fear of failure in particular, is a much bigger issue in today's world. Take LinkedIn for example: our professional credentials, achievements and success, or lack thereof – are there for all the world to see. Meanwhile, with Instagram and even Snapchat, we're stuck in a habit of social comparison. You might not even realise it but if you're active on social media, you may be constantly comparing yourself to others; we measure our achievements and failures against someone else's. And it's not just professional successes we're comparing, it's personal too. But of course it's all perceived. 'She appears to be living a more successful life than me.' Naturally, because everything is now more public and more measured, there's a reluctance to put yourself out there in case of public failure; this has certainly affected my self-confidence. And what could be more public than writing a book for all the world (or at least someone other than my mother) to read?

At the same time, it's interesting to note that with some of the most successful people in the world speaking out about their less than favourable grades in school (Simon Cowell) or their lack of interest in doing what they were told (Richard Branson bailed on school at the age of sixteen) or their experience of having fallen on hard times (J.K. Rowling jumps to mind for this one), things are changing. We're realising that there are several routes to success and it's not just about everything we're taught in school. It's not that we should all give up and flounder, kick back and hope that we just land on our feet some day. Remember, the people behind such success stories might not have been book smart but they had self-belief and other necessary traits to succeed in spades.

Maybe we should change or at least loosen our perception of failure. This is a relatively new way of thinking. For so long, there was nothing good about failure, so it makes total sense that we'd fear it. But in my lifetime, the ground has begun to shift and perhaps future generations won't be brought up with the same aversion to failure. We're certainly far removed from the days when failure in school meant a literal slap on the wrist. We're only very recently looking at failure in a more fair and positive light, as a stepping stone to greater things and as a necessary learning curve for a life of fulfilment.

How does modern life play into a fear of failure?

According to Dr Aisling Leonard-Curtin,[20] 'The fact that our successes and failures are so public nowadays really ups the stakes for many people. Now if we succeed or fail, these moments can be uploaded to a wide variety of social media platforms, which gives us the chance to relive these successes or failures whether we want to or not. For many of us, the thought of failing so publicly is far from appealing. Rather, our red alert threat system becomes activated. If we have failed in the past, we may relive this experience again and again and again.

We know from psychological research that people are far more disinhibited about how they comment online. Whilst there is a chance that someone might say something insensitive to you about a failure in person, these chances are relatively slim. Online, everyone feels entitled to their voice and their views on any success or failure. There can be a thought process along the lines of "well, if they've put it up here, I can say whatever I want". As such, people often make far more hurtful comments online than they would make in person. Such hurtful comments can really fuel a shame cycle for the person who is already trying to come to grips with a failure that was difficult for them to experience and process in the first place. A shame cycle can lead to the person defining themselves, rather than their actions, as a failure. This can make it harder for people to get back to engaging in the actions they need to succeed in the future.

Although there is a different phenomenon around success, there can be very similar processes. Online, some people will try to bring someone down a "peg or two" who is deemed successful. On the flipside, if you have had a success and the responses are overwhelmingly positive and supportive, this can also lead to some difficulty psychologically as many will buy into the belief that they need to maintain that level of momentum to hold on to their success.

Psychological tip: It is best to notice what thoughts, emotions and bodily sensations arise for you when you get some feedback online, regardless of whether you deem it positive or negative. As best you can, simply notice this as a comment rather than allowing it to define you. It can be flattering to buy into all the positive hype, however if your self-worth is contingent on what other people think of you, this sets you up for a fall later on. Similarly, if you buy into the unfavourable things that people say about you, you may avoid engaging in actions that would be very helpful for you.

So, it is best to notice your internal responses, come back to what's important to you and let this be your guide rather than a desire to elicit some particular responses in others and avoid other responses deemed negative to you.'

Understanding Confidence

What is confidence?

Though you find this chapter relatively early in this book, it's one that I put off writing for as long as I could, such is the challenge of defining confidence. It's tough because to fully understand confidence, we also have to tease out self-esteem and courage (and even competence), and things can get very confusing very quickly. While these attributes are often interchangeable, they are, in fact, different concepts and the distinction is important. For the most part, we use the word 'confidence' as an umbrella term for all three, but for the purposes of this particular chapter, I'm going to drill down a little further so we're super clear.

In the most simple terms, confidence is being sure of *yourself* and your abilities in specific areas (in psychology terms, confidence is 'domain specific' and relates to a specific thing or action). I put an emphasis on 'yourself' there, because this is quite different to being sure of the *outcome* (which is impossible, unless you have psychic abilities).

The word 'confidence' comes from the Latin *fidere* which means 'to trust'. Being sure of yourself, regardless of the outcome, is more doable than predicting the future. Confidence builds first and foremost through practical experience. But perhaps, more importantly, it develops with a practised mindset. What I mean here is that it's partly born of experience (i.e. based on facts – for example, someone might say, 'I've given ten talks now and I know, based on how those ten have gone, that I will be more than competent to do it again), and partly about having the faith in yourself to take the leap before you've gained the experience at all (i.e. 'I've never done this before, but I believe I will get through it'). And this is the real clincher. It's about being okay with *all* probabilities, good and bad. Psychotherapist Mark Tyrrell terms this 'comfortable neutrality'.[21]

According to Tyrrell, we should stop looking for a feeling of total confidence before we do something for the first time. Sometimes, it requires courage (proceeding when you are fearful), but with comfortable neutrality, we can fast track ourselves towards confidence. For him, comfortable neutrality (which is allowing yourself to relax with the idea of not knowing what the outcome will be and being open-minded) plus experience equals confidence. Let that sink in:

Comfortable neutrality + experience = confidence

This is the kind of practical thinking I like, rather than the airy-fairy sentiments such as 'positive thinking equals success'.

Now, let's explore what confidence is *not* – or, rather, my interpretation of what it is not. As there are many myths surrounding confidence, I'm going to hone in on just a few that I feel are important.

1. Confidence is not a personality type
It's not being an extrovert or being really social or loud or popular. You may be all of these things and still not be confident. You can be an incredibly confident person and still be an introvert and not the most sociable person in your gang. I know plenty of insecure extroverts and confident introverts. Confidence is an attribute that can come about with all personalities. You can absolutely gain more confidence without a drastic change in your personality, so we can leave the lobotomy for another day.

2. Confidence is not about being better than anyone else
It's not about being the most competent person in the

room, it's a quiet, inner knowledge that you are capable. As explained by psychotherapist Mark Tyrrell, a truly confident person doesn't think they're great or spend too long self-analysing. Typically, they are more attuned to what they are doing than wondering what others are thinking of them. 'Socially confident people, for example, focus outwards onto others rather than inward (even to think: "Aren't I great?").' So if someone can't get enough of themselves in the mirror, this does not suggest they are confident.

3. Confidence isn't the same as vanity

In that same sense, if you think the person attracting the most attention is the most confident, you're probably wrong. Before we go any further, get the clichéd idea of a confident person as someone empirically attractive sashaying across a room and attracting everyone's attention out of your head. This warped idea of confidence – and all the myths that go with it – comes at us from all angles of the media. In reality, it might actually be the quiet one in the corner who's focused on what she's doing who is the most sure of herself.

4. Confidence is not a fixed and unchanging thing

We're not born with it (contrary to what Maybelline might suggest). Instead, we cultivate it through experience. It's an outcome. When you describe yourself as someone who lacks self-confidence, this is not a true or definitive statement about you as a person. It may be where you feel you are right now, but it's not a given that this is the way you are going to be from here on out (if you are willing to experience new situations and new environments). So with this in mind, stop putting destructive labels on yourself. All that does is reinforce unhelpful behaviour that keeps success out of reach.

5. Even when we have confidence, it can be transient

In my experience, confidence can definitely ebb and flow. Sometimes, I feel like I can take on the world and, if I really put my mind to it, I could just 'decide' to become a multimillionaire by next week. And that's because I've put my mind to things before and they've worked out (none of which have made me a multimillionaire). Other times, I wish my mother was a kangaroo so I could hide inside her belly pouch. The most confident people in the world don't feel confident all of the time and will grapple with their fair share of insecurities. They are not always certain that things will work out. What they will do, however, is move forward in spite of their fears.

6. Confidence is not an all-or-nothing state of being

You're not wholly confident or entirely lacking in confidence at any one time: you might be greatly sure in one area of your life but significantly uncertain in another, and this is common to most of us. Come to think of it, I'm not sure a single person exists who is confident in every aspect of their life all of the time. If there is, they're probably bored out of their tree. There'd be nothing left to learn and no room for growth – so let's not aim for that. Just as there can be no person who is completely confident in everything they do, so there is no such thing as an entirely unconfident person (remember, we all have a comfort zone).

7. You do not have to be successful in order to be confident
It can actually work the other way around in that we tend to reach success by developing confidence, which requires courage, and believing that we have what it takes to get there. Otherwise, we probably wouldn't be motivated to bother, would we?

Perhaps most important and relevant to this book is the myth about fearlessness.

8. Neither confidence nor courage should be defined as fearlessness
From the beginning of time to this moment right now, the human experience has been punctuated by fear (it's what's kept us alive), yet there are still those among us who are, for the most part, very confident people. So know this: fear and confidence coexist. I've learned these past few years that fear is a necessary stepping stone towards confidence, which, in turn, brings us to success.

What's more, just as confidence is not a life without fear, it's also not the absence of failure. True confidence requires a willingness to fail, fail fast, fail again and fail better until you get it right. A confident person is relaxed with uncertainty and okay with failure.

Courage

We're all familiar with the idea of moving forwards in spite of fear. We call this confidence, but technically it's courage and, arguably, it's more important than confidence. Why? Because it's what comes first. It's what we need to take action. In other words, it's what we need *until* we have confidence. Confidence and courage interplay with one another, and while we regularly conflate the two, courage is what we employ when we *don't* feel confident, when we feel scared and unsure. Courage steps in and takes over the reins in the absence of confidence.

Typically, we all need a certain amount of courage to begin something new – when we are faced with something outside of our comfort zone – because our minds respond to uncertainty with fear. Confidence, on the other hand, is what we get as a result of being courageous.

Generally speaking, the more confident we become, the less we need to invoke our courage.

To better understand the difference between the two – because, for me, it can be a bit of a head scratcher – I was told a story of two men who jumped into a river to save their friend. One had courage and one had confidence. The one with courage was very scared of swimming but jumped in anyway. The other was confident in his swimming abilities but underestimated the current. They both drowned (which is far from the uplifting story you were hoping for and I was never told what happened to the third man – but you get the difference, a burst of courage can compensate for a lack of confidence in the short term). Unlike confidence, courage requires strength, and if you develop your courage (which is essentially feeling the fear and doing it anyway), your confidence will grow, and as a result your fear of failure will shrivel down to nothing more than a bit of background noise.

You might think you lack confidence, but you don't necessarily lack courage. In Part Two, we look at the building blocks for confidence, for which, at times, courage is a major, major requirement.

Elon Musk is one of the most influential businessmen in the world (you might have heard of him, he's the man behind Tesla, who aims to build a colony on Mars within a decade – no big deal). Facing multimillion-dollar decisions on a daily basis (we're talking hernia-inducing stress for the likes of me), Musk could easily be the poster boy for 'fearlessness'. Look at what he's willing to try and to risk with his various professional endeavours. But in reality, he's anything but. He has spoken with candour of his struggles with the fear of failure – not in a woe-is-me kind of way, but in a this-is-what-normal-life-is way; it's not anything to feel bad about or try to change. 'I feel fear quite strongly,' he says during a filmed interview with Sam Altman of Y Combinator.[22] The confidence he has built comes partly from experience, a belief that he's on to something brilliant and, at the same time, a willingness to accept that sometimes in life failure is going to present itself. Ultimately, he's okay with uncertainty (comfortable neutrality), he has enough faith in himself and whatever happens, he'll handle it. That is confidence.

Musk also says in this interview, 'There are times when something is important enough, you believe in it enough, that you do it in spite of fear.'

This takes me back to one of my favourite quotations, one that I always return to when I'm feeling really uncertain and I'm about to take a leap into the unknown: 'Let your faith be bigger than your fear.' It doesn't have to be a religious faith but faith in yourself.

Musk inspires one of the essential tools in my confidence kit that you will find in Part Two: fear hacking (or fatalism) that, in short, is all about being okay with the worst-case scenario. It's not as bleak as it sounds, in fact it's very powerful. Musk says, 'If you accept the probabilities, that diminishes fear.' For Musk, neither confidence nor courage is about fearlessness or farting rainbows, it's what happens when you feel the fear, employ a coping strategy (stay tuned for Part Two) to get through it and do it anyway.

Confidence is a skill that we can all develop.

What I'm hoping you're getting from this is that confidence isn't something that one person possesses and another person doesn't. It's a skill that every single one of us can develop. Sometimes, we rely more on courage than confidence – and perhaps you'll consider courage a more noble attribute – but both bring us towards success, which we'll start defining in a moment. Yes, certain people will naturally find it easier to be confident and more courageous than others – maybe they've just put themselves out there and failed more often – but we can all learn and improve if we're willing to try. Above all else, I really encourage you to wrap your head around the fact that confidence needn't ever be about the absence of fear. It's about being okay with fear and okay with the idea of failure. And that's why trying to become fearless is a pointless exercise that you should give up right now.

I now use my feelings of fear before I do something new and nerve-racking as a great motivator. It's so part of my routine to feel fearful and as though my intestines are doing the Mexican wave that I'd almost feel weird if it wasn't there. I expect it, I recognise it, I tap into my courage reserves and my confidence grows as a result. And that pre-game fear helps me do a better job, I'm convinced of it. When it comes to something new that gives my amygdala palpitations, my mother describes me as a shark (though sometimes I feel more like plankton), circling around the thing that I want, before going in for the kill. That sounds like a shark with a lot of compassion and empathy for what's about to become its dinner, but you get the gist.

Confidence v competence

So we know that confidence is something that we can learn, but here's another question: Is it something we can fake? Is there power in 'fake it till you make it', as the saying goes?

Some people think true confidence cannot be forced, but others would beg to differ. To a certain extent, I believe that true and lasting confidence follows experience and repetition, but you can get considerably far in your endeavours with a few simple tricks to help create the physiology of confidence. For example, by adopting high-power poses and puffing out your chest for two minutes (as opposed to hunching over and making yourself appear smaller), Amy Cuddy (whose 2012 TED Talk is a must-watch) and her fellow Harvard researchers[23] found an increase in testosterone, which is said to make us feel powerful, while, at the same time, they recorded a decrease in cortisol, the stress hormone, thus giving us a self-made dose of 'you've got this' from the simple act of chest-puffing. In this sense, confidence might even matter more than actual competence. This comes up a lot in interviews and important business meetings. Look around, it's not always the person with the most boxes ticked on their CV that gets the role or rises up the ranks, but rather the person who appears to have boundless belief in themselves, whether this is genuine or not.

If you're a pilot or a surgeon, you need as much competence as you do confidence, obviously. I don't want the person operating on my brain to be taking a leap into the unknown or to say, 'I think I can do this.' But in certain situations, such as a job interview or in a social situation, confidence can take the lead.

According to one Hewlett-Packard study published in *The McKinsey Quarterly* in 2008,[24] men would ask for a promotion when they met a mere 60 per cent of the new role's requirements. They were confident by nature. Women, on the other hand, would only step forward when they had every box ticked and knew that, on paper at least, they were a perfect fit. They prioritised competence. They only felt confident when they were competent. Who was more likely to get the promotion? The men, of course. This opens up another can of worms: the confidence gap between men and women, which is a very real thing and important to consider. (I tease this out further in Chapter 7)

Whether confidence or competence matters more will vary from person to person, but from what I've read, it seems they come together in a chicken-and-egg sort of scenario. In psychology circles, it's referred to as the confidence/competence loop (and get set for a series of tongue-twisters).

We increase our confidence as we increase our competence, gaining knowledge in a particular area and developing our skills. This gives us what's called 'competence-confidence'. (If, however, we don't reach competence-confidence, we may be maladaptively perfectionistic - which is a whole other conversation, explored in Chapter 6). The women in the Hewlett-Packard study were (and this is a generalisation) waiting until they had competence-confidence. But we also increase our competence (which is defined purely as the ability to do something efficiently) when we increase our self-confidence. The men in HP were willing to let the competence come later.

Self-confidence and competence-confidence aren't the same thing, though, again, these are terms that are lumped together for convenience. With the former, you are confident that you will be able to do something when you don't necessarily have the skills; you know that you will go out and get the skills. It's a belief in yourself. Whereas competence-confidence is something we only get with experience. With true self-confidence, you are okay with the fact that you might not have the skills or know the outcome.

Still with me?

Where things become detrimental, however, is when you see your lack of skills as evidence of your lack of worth.

Self-Worth
And Success

LET'S TALK ABOUT our sense of self-worth because this is *very* important. If your head is starting to feel like it's full of cauliflower after all that rambling about confidence and courage and competence, take a quick break and come back to me. I'll take one too. This next part deserves every ounce of our focus.

...

Aaaand we're back. Let's go.

How we measure our worth and how we view ourselves is the crux of this whole thing - confidence, courage, the fear of failure, success - everything. For me, a person's self-confidence and ability to act courageously at any given time will depend on what they think about themselves and the beliefs they hold about themselves and their character.

This is your self-esteem, which, again, just to make things extra complicated, is not quite the same as self-confidence – it's sometimes called your self-worth.

Self-confidence is linked with action. It's all wrapped up in doing something (remember we used the term 'domain specific'?), whereas self-esteem is more general. It's how you see yourself in the world – are you a worthwhile human being? It's the opinion you have about yourself and it's just sort of there in the background. It's not something you think about on a daily basis and it doesn't tend to change without conscious work, but that's not to say it's entirely inflexible. 'Esteem' derives from the Latin *aestimare*, meaning to appraise, value or estimate, and, according to Dr Neel Burton, author of *Heaven and Hell: The Psychology of the Emotions*,[25] self-esteem is our cognitive and emotional appraisal of our own worth, the basis of which varies from person to person.

One person's self-esteem may be based on receiving approval from others. For someone else, it might be based on their work. For another again, it might be based on the loving relationships in their life. When developing your self-confidence, it's useful to check in on your self-esteem. If you have healthy self-esteem (i.e. you think you are worthy and good enough and you love yourself regardless of your achievements), your confidence will grow more easily as a result.

What's the difference between having healthy or low self-esteem? Psychotherapist Mark Tyrrell[26] says that if you have the former, you will see failure (such as a failed job interview or a relationship break-up) as relating to the specifics (i.e. 'the relationship just wasn't working anymore' or 'I didn't have the skills required for that particular job') and it doesn't reflect on you as a person. On the other hand, if you have low self-esteem, you will spread this negative event across everything (i.e. 'What is wrong with me?', 'My life is a disaster', 'I am crap', 'I'm destined to stay where I am', 'I can't cope with anything', etc.). 'In this way,' explains Tyrrell, 'we can see that there is a kind of extremism, a black-and-white, all-or-nothing type of thinking to low self-esteem.'

I have found myself in post-failure scenarios (where something hasn't gone the way I had hoped) questioning myself as a person. This is not good.

At the same time, note the use of the term 'healthy self-esteem' as opposed to 'high self-esteem'. Tyrrell explains that self-esteem doesn't have to be particularly high as high self-esteem is usually coupled with low impulse control and it's what you might see in someone that we would describe as psychopathic. 'Going around thinking you are automatically wonderful (and therefore everything must be someone else's fault) is as much a way of misusing the imagination as low self-esteem.'

It can be just as counter-productive. He continues, 'Self-esteem is really a by-product of meeting your emotional needs and having a healthy sense of self-observation and self-reflection about yourself that is realistic and calm.' So if you observe yourself as a whole in the wake of something going wrong, chances are you won't be too kind. Instead, focus on the specifics. Now, there are definitely people who are confident and also have low self-esteem (think of some famous performers) but, typically, confidence will come a lot more easily if you have your self-esteem in a healthy place. What's more, if you get this part right, the fear of failure won't be as big an issue.

Ask yourself
If I fail or succeed on this, is it linked to my sense of self-worth?

Ultimately, you need to assess whether or not failing or succeeding in something specific is linked with your sense of worth. Know this: like insecurity in relationships, the fear of failure will absolutely increase when we feel that to fail is a reflection of who we are as a person. Some people, explains Tyrrell, attach their whole sense of worth to just about everything they do or every interaction they have. Is this you? Don't worry, I also am in the process of making sure it's not me. It's hard. Undoing this habit can be a bit of an art form.

Whether or not you fail in a specific challenge shouldn't change how you see yourself. To get a sense of your self-esteem and how you measure your self-worth, ask yourself what matters the most to you and how you define success. If the answer lies in professional achievements, things get tricky. If you feel that your life has meaning and that you are happy when you succeed but that when you don't, you feel worthless, you need to realign your values. Because life is an inevitable series of high points and low points with lots of averages in between. This will be a constant roadblock for you. (Jump to Chapter 20 where we explore handling failure in more detail.) This doesn't have to mean that professional goals don't matter – they matter a lot to me – but they don't make me the inherently good (I hope) and worthwhile person that I am. If you value yourself when things are bad as much as you do when things are good, managing failure becomes a lot easier while confidence becomes less elusive and a lot more tangible.

Exercise

VISUALISATION EXERCISE
....

I do this exercise when I need to get my emotional ducks back in a row, it helps me get a healthier perspective on my self-worth. I imagine a shield around myself. On the inside, I have my core – my self-worth – and it's protected. Here, I believe that I have value in the world and that I am worthy. Here, you'll also find my core values, which are the driving force in my life. These are the fundamental choices of who I want to be and how I view myself. They could include things like having meaningful relationships, having great empathy for others and having integrity in everything I do. These are things that I can control.

One of the things that is most important to me these days is my health. Having experienced crippling anxiety to the point that nothing gave me joy, I have a newfound perspective on what really matters, and, for me, that's feeling well. When I didn't appreciate how important my health was, I would easily have prioritised a career that wasn't just satisfying but also looked good on the outside. If that's at the centre of me, I'm on shaky ground. But back to my shield! This is the ideal. On the outside of it, I can experience failure and success but both of these should bounce off the shield and never be able to penetrate within, either chipping off a piece of my self-worth (in the case of failure) or enhancing it (in the case of success). If, on the other hand, I measure myself against my professional success and I allow it to be a core value of mine, I'm back to that roadblock. This is an external event in my life and something that I cannot control. Core values shouldn't be things that you cannot control.

What is success?

Let's gather ourselves. We've been talking a lot about success and I have yet to attempt to define it. There are two layers of success, I think. Success is sometimes defined as the good outcome of an undertaking. On one level, we measure our whole lives in terms of success, with life itself being the ultimate undertaking. Did we lead a successful life? Was it a good life? Did we achieve what we set out to achieve? Then, there are the micro-level, day-to-day undertakings, some more significant than others. For example, going to the gym and having a satisfying workout is a success. Giving a talk, not face-planting and feeling proud of myself for a job well done is a success. In this sense, success is the accomplishment of an aim.

Beyond these two measures, success is entirely open to interpretation. It varies from person to person. By most people's standards, we associate success with tangible achievements, such as getting a promotion, having a high-flying career, getting paid lots of money, working our way up the ladder, having a lot to show for our efforts. Money and power are the traditional markers of success, because of what we're taught in school and the structures within our society, as well as the ways in which they're portrayed in the media. To be blunt, for a good many of us, if you're rich, you're successful. If, for you, success is linked to money and what your CV looks like and a long list of achievements, that's normal. We're all conditioned to interpret success in this way so, as always, don't be too hard on yourself.

I would be lying if I said that the thought of lots of money in my bank account didn't feel like success. For some people, though, success is less about what you can hold in your hand. Instead, it equals contentment. (Note: I don't use the word *happiness* because I think contentment is a high enough aim, whereas happiness is a little more elusive.)

Success can be as simple as liking yourself, being surrounded by good people whom you love and who love you, enjoying what you do on a daily basis, appreciating the small things in life, maybe feeling that you are making a contribution to the world, being healthy, being able to sleep well, and feeling physically and emotionally well. For some people, these are the real achievements in life, and if you satisfy these, you will feel accomplished. The day-to-day successes and failures come and go, but it's with these metrics that their picture of true success is drawn.

There is another, less discussed definition of success that matters a lot to me, and it's what's inspired this book in the first place: personal development.

On one hand, personal development is critical for success – it's why we're here working through this book – but on the other hand, personal development *is* success. Yes, being content is the mother of all successes, but facing the challenges of day-to-day life, whether they involve money, career or other things, contributes towards our personal development. After all, you can be content and never challenge yourself or develop as a person, so as far as I'm concerned, personal development is up there with contentment.

In her bestselling book *Thrive*, Arianna Huffington (of *The Huffington Post*) argues that we need to look beyond money and power as signifiers of success and instead implement a system that features 'four pillars', as she describes them: wisdom, well-being, wonder and giving.[27]

To me, these pillars could all live under the umbrella of personal development and, money aside, they are the motivators behind most of what we take on.

The easiest way to figure out what true success really means to you is to ask yourself: 'What in life brings me joy?' Is it the challenge of making more money? Or does that make you feel stressed? Does the feeling of knowing you've overcome a fear or learned something give you joy? It does for me. Does prioritising your health give you joy? This will always be top of my list. Is it about making a difference in people's lives? Is it about what you get or what you become? There are many ways to approach success. Another way to distil your definition of success comes via the author of *The Seven Habits of Highly Effective People*, Stephen Covey: 'If you carefully consider what you want to be said of you in the funeral experience, you will find your definition of success.'[28] So, though it's grim, think about this for a minute.

With your bigger, macro sense of 'true success' locked down, there's still plenty of room for enjoying and appreciating the daily challenges that drive us and motivate us, for which we need self-confidence. If you suddenly lost your appetite for this kind of success, well, the rest of this book would be pretty redundant.

Remember: Macro is the bigger picture. You can achieve micro successes without it affecting your macro-level success. It depends how you grade your macro-level success. Is this task important to you in terms of macro success? Will it matter in five years' time?

Things that you may be using to measure your self-worth

The following is a list of determinants you may be using to measure your self-worth, which, ideally, you shouldn't use at all. The thing is, however, that we all turn to them from time to time. I certainly do. We can easily fall into a trap where we start to look at our appearance as a measure of how good we are or we feel really deflated about ourselves as a person when we hear that someone is making more money than we are. This is like aiming at a target that's constantly moving because these things are all changeable. If your self-worth is linked to money, for example, and you compare yourself to others, and you feel that you are more valuable than the person with nothing, how will you feel about yourself when that person becomes a millionaire overnight? Do you see how quickly and dramatically your perception of yourself could change?

This is important. The goal isn't to beat yourself up about this even more, like 'this is just something else I'm doing wrong'. That would be absolutely counterproductive. Instead, just observe which traps you might fall into and go easy on yourself. You can reprogramme your thinking in such a way that the following can certainly be important to you, but not the driving force of your life. These are external factors. If you have healthy self-esteem, they shouldn't determine your worth or your success. If any of these things were to change tomorrow, your self-worth should remain intact. Whether or not they determine how good a person you are is a choice.

1. Your appearance

Unfortunately, beauty has long been tied to self-worth. The entire fashion and beauty (and sometimes health) industries are dependent on it. Across the world, we're conditioned to believe that we're only as good as we look. Looking good can certainly enhance your confidence in certain situations and it gives you a boost, but should your self-worth be dependent on a good hair day?

It will be really hard to undo this link if it's the only way we measure our self-worth and if it's a major determinant for our mood. This is especially hard because we live in a world that favours beauty, and social media really doesn't help (I have written before about feeling low after consuming an entire feed of perfectly filtered gym-bunny selfies). It's important not to confuse the short-term confidence boost that you might get from, say, your favourite pair of jeans with how you feel about yourself as a person.

What's the best way to wean ourselves off this pattern? For one, I find limiting my social media scrolling helps a lot. Decide what beauty is to you, in the body that you have, instead of letting the world tell you. Unless you're going to go under the knife, which still might not make you feel more worthy, you're stuck in the skin that you've got. I appreciate that it will take time for this to change in your mind – and I have definitely had days where a spot the size of Krakatoa has made me feel insignificant as a person – but write it down for yourself: Is it really about having a golden tan? Is it having perfect skin? Or could it be relative to only you and be about taking care of yourself and being healthy? The latter is a more helpful way to look at things because it hones in on just you rather than comparing yourself to others, which is almost never a good idea.

Write it down: 'My self-worth is not attached to my looks.'

2. Your net worth

You are not more or less worthy depending on how much money you have in your bank account, even though, again, we've been conditioned to associate wealth with being more important. The poorest person can have the same self-esteem and sense of value as a multimillionaire. If your value correlates to the amount of money you have, will you ever have enough? The more money we have, the more possessions we acquire, but ask anyone who's ever won the lottery – it's a short-term high and then you just become used to it. The same problems (that aren't financial problems, of course) will still be there when you've got a fat wallet. Similarly, if you lost all of your money tomorrow, you wouldn't be worthless as a person.

Write it down: 'My self-worth is not determined by my net worth.'

3. What people think about you

This one's a biggie. There are so many articles out there telling you how to stop caring about what other people think of you. But the fact is that most of us *do* care and there are several good reasons for this.

First of all, we aren't born with a sense of self or a sense of self-worth, that comes later (when our cognitive abilities have developed – one study says we develop a sense of self from the age of five)[29] and so we create a picture of who we are and what we are like based on other people – our parents, our siblings, our friends, our teachers. In a way, our perception of ourselves is based on our perception of how we think others perceive us, if you will. If we didn't care about what people think at all, we probably wouldn't be as considerate or as kind to others. We are social creatures by nature, so it's important to have a reaction when, for example, we hurt or offend somebody. This has helped us progress as a society, especially when it comes to people we care about. Caring about your loved ones inherently involves caring about what they think, and that's okay. In fact, it makes you a better person to a certain extent.

The key is caring what other people think, i.e. not being an asshole, while, at the same time, not allowing what other people think to dominate your self-perception (which is easier to do when you realign your values and your own measures of self-worth, which we'll get to). This is why it's important to take the time to really look inward and make an assessment for yourself and know your own mind. Otherwise, we will continue to try to please others as a way to validate ourselves and let others guide our actions.

Things go awry when we care too much, and if you're anything like me, you are definitely guilty of overestimating just how much time other people spend thinking about you. Though it sounds rude, when my friends have issues (and it's always easier to give advice than to take advice, I know that), and they're worrying about what other people will think to the point that it's holding them back from making a decision that will serve them well, I try to gently remind them that others will probably give it a few moments of their time, express their judgement if at all and then go straight back to their own world. These things rarely affect other people as much as we think they will – but it affects us hugely.

Think about it: you're reading this right now wondering what other people think about you and whether or not you really care what other people think about you. What you're not thinking about is what you think about other people. Caring too much, attaching it to our self-worth and overestimating others is to our own detriment. If your self-esteem can rise and fall depending on what people think about you - which, again, is external - you're in for a bumpy ride. I had an experience quite recently where I learned that someone who I don't know at all didn't like me, for reasons unknown. I really struggled to let it go, saying 'but I'm nice!' but, eventually, by reminding myself of what and who matters to me, I've been able to move past it.

To some extent, I'll always care about what the people I care about think of me, but I don't need to be concerned with the wider public (read: total randomers). Be careful not to confuse this with not caring about other people. You don't have to know someone well to care about them as another human being. What I'm talking about here specifically is caring about what other people *think of you*. So, for example, it's normal and okay to want the approval of your nearest and dearest, provided you are your own person. It only becomes a problem when, for example, your fear of what total strangers will think about your performance stops you from doing it or you don't go for it with the love of your life because others might think you're doomed to fail. Unless you're hurting someone else in the process, ask yourself what you would do if you took other people's opinions out of the equation.

We all have that person to whom we say, 'Your opinion means the most to me.' Try saying it in front of the mirror instead. If you're a people-pleaser – I am too! – it's time to strengthen your sense of self.

Signs of a people-pleaser:
- You find yourself agreeing, or at least pretending to agree, with others
- You apologise a lot when you've done nothing wrong
- You have a very hard time saying no
- You take everyone else's feelings on board, as though it's your responsibility
- You put others' wants and needs ahead of yours
- You really struggle with any kind of social confrontation – an argument with a friend, for example
- If you're hurt in a situation, you might not speak up about it because you don't want to make anyone else feel bad

The same goes for who you know. You shouldn't feel more valuable because you are in with the popular crowd; this is a major issue for teenagers and this is one thing the movies get right: you know the story, a kid becomes accepted into the 'cool' gang and feel that they've finally made it and that those on the 'outside' are 'losers'. It gets a lot easier and definitely less black and white as you become an adult, but we can still easily fall into a similar trap in other, more subtle, ways. People whose worth depends on the appraisal of others will struggle with confidence, because what people think about you is outside of your control.

Write it down: 'My value is not determined by other people.'

4. What you achieve

A lot of conversations start with the most recent thing we've achieved – it's just one of those go-to topics, like the weather. But to measure ourselves against our achievements is like building a house on quicksand. Again, this thinking is set in stone from an early age when we are rewarded for achieving something in school. Our parents tell us how proud they are of us and, of course, this is encouraging and lovely to hear – but this is where the link is made between achievements and worth.

Naturally, parents are just trying to motivate their children and if success doesn't come with some sort of reward, we wouldn't try to succeed. But we need to be told by our parents as kids that they are proud of us for the people we are and for trying and for effort, not just for succeeding. We need to be told we're loved and valued and this needs to be reinforced even when we've failed or missed the grade. Otherwise, no wonder we develop a strong fear of failure. And, of course, as we get older, the things we could fail at get bigger. Now, it's not just your two times tables but your job that pays the money that buys the food, and so on and so forth.

If someone has had more failures than successes, they are not less than the person who's had more successes than failures - but that is hard to believe when we've been conditioned to think the opposite. If the only way to feel good about ourselves is to experience continued success via these kinds of external achievements, we're bound to experience significant lows when things don't go our way. What can we do? Absolutely, feel proud of your accomplishments and enjoy them, but know that they are a temporary peak and, ideally, you should return to a normal state of being that feels good, that isn't affected by achievement or lack thereof.

Write it down: 'My value is not attached to my medals and awards and straight As. I am still of value when I fail.'

5. Your relationship status

This is a topic that could become a whole other book, such is my rage about what society is telling us. This is a hard one (for women, mostly) because, for most of us, our relationships matter more than anything – so how can we not be massively affected by them? How can we not put so much weight on our relationships when, if we're single, we're asked whether or not we've found 'the one' or 'that special someone'? Well, we are 'the one', goddammit.

If we're single in our late twenties or early thirties, we're told not to worry because 'there's still time'. Time to lock down the ultimate qualifier of worth before you shrivel up and die. I wish the world would stop telling us this. Maybe by the time I have grandkids (which, again, won't determine my worth) they'll have an easier time of it. Women have moved on significantly since we depended on a partner for financial security but society is still beating this message over our heads with a stick. Until it catches up, we can work on our own internal narratives. That, at least, we can change. Relationships that are good can enhance your life, adding to your experience in a positive way, and we all gravitate towards partnerships, but they shouldn't be the foundation on which your happiness is built. This is yet another belief system deeply ingrained into our subconscious. If your relationship ended tomorrow, would you be less worthy?

Do you believe that having a partner is the ultimate goal in life? Have you been watching too much *Sex and the City* and firmly believe that being single is a plight?

Though it sounds like a cliché, you need to accept and love yourself before anyone else comes into the picture. You need to remind yourself that you are fiercely independent and require no security from another person. It's as simple as that.

It took me a long time to stop seeing my relationship status as a measure of my value. As a teenager, I felt I was nothing until I had a boyfriend (too many movies, peer pressure). When I broke up with my first love after a six-year whirlwind of hormonal extremes, I was inconsolable (as is the case for every half-teen/half-demon). The pain and intensity of emotion in your late teens/ early twenties can be excruciating, though I look back on it now with a more balanced perspective. At the time, he was so wrapped up in my self-worth that, without him, I felt broken (world's tiniest violin, please). It would have been natural and easy to fill that void with someone else but I was scared of ever going through that pain again, and I began to realise (I don't know where it came from) that it wasn't good for me to attach so much significance to a boyfriend. I'd always be miserable, in love and out of love. So I built myself up over a long time until I felt content to be on my own. Only when I felt I was a whole person was I able to let someone else into my life. He's the man I'm going to marry and I love him with every ounce of my being. So I'm sorry, Jerry Maguire, but I am already complete.

> **Write it down: 'My value is not attached to my relationship status.'**

Exercise
SELF-COMPASSION

Write down a list of things you'd say to a friend – e.g. 'you're doing great' or 'we'll still love you if it doesn't work out' or 'have faith in yourself' – and, once written, re-read them as though they weren't for a friend, but just for you.

6. Your social media status

This sounds trivial but I don't doubt there are now millions of young women (and perhaps men too) who allow their social media to be a determining factor of their self-worth. It's a generational thing and it's a new medium for comparing ourselves to others and allowing what other people think about us to affect us.

How many likes did your last post get? How many people viewed your story? How many followers have you gained? Have you lost any followers? Did a post not do as well as you thought it would? Do you feel less than the person who has thousands of followers?

This is a real problem today and you might laugh at the idea that 'likes' could have this effect on how we feel about ourselves but it is now so ingrained into our daily routine, it can enhance or detract from our mood. My partner has the best attitude to social media: he just doesn't use it. He doesn't care and he doesn't think he's missing out on anything important. He calls the friends that he values on the phone and he couldn't give a tuppenny f*ck about getting the approval of a hundred people that he's never met and never will. I'm not suggesting you take his extreme approach – I enjoy Instagram – but be mindful of letting it slip in through the cracks in your shield. Use social media for what it is – if you catch yourself on a high because of a successful post or feeling low because five people mysteriously unfollowed you, go back to your list of what really matters to you.

Write it down: 'Social media is fun but it doesn't mean sh*t.'

Exercise

SOCIAL MEDIA DETOX

If you find yourself measuring your self-worth against your social media successes, try this: Hide or even delete your social media apps for a week (when/if you re-download the app, your account details will have been saved) and see what a difference it makes to your life. Do you feel slightly more in control and happier in your own life without constantly looking at what other people are buying/wearing/eating? Do you feel a sort of relief? What, really, have you missed?

If there is anything else that you've used to measure your self-worth, write it down and get a clear sense of where you stand right now. How you define your values and how you've defined success up until now. How have you measured how well you are doing? Does it involve sizing yourself up against others? Is it all outward? Be brutally honest with yourself.

If you measure your self-worth on what your boss says to you, for example, then consider the very likely fact that they may be having a sh*t day and are just in a bad mood – just like any other human being on the planet. Maybe, just before you walked in, they got some bad news. Or maybe they are just a complete asshole for whom berating their staff is top of management 101. Who knows? Regardless, it shows that putting so much importance into feedback from other people in terms of our self-worth is giving them too much control. Take back control of your self-worth. Be the boss of your own self-worth.

Things that could be used to measure your self-worth instead

Now that we have covered the main culprits that are typically used to determine our self-esteem, let's consider what might be a healthier option. If, instead, you use the following as a measure of your self-worth, you will find confidence comes easier.

These are the kind of things that will still matter when you're old and grey, looking back over the life you've lived. These are things you can control – they are internal factors, governed by you – that are far more stable than any of the determinants we've covered previously. For example, if your self-worth is partly composed of your ability to love, this won't change about you if your relationship comes to an end or if you weren't in one to begin with. Get it?

Here are some other things that are a more positive way of measuring your self-worth:
○ the way you treat people
○ your ability to care about other people

- having empathy
- how you handle tough times
- how much love you give
- being a supportive person
- being reliable
- being an honest person
- being a loyal person
- having integrity and being authentic
- having a clear sense of right and wrong
- valuing justice and having a strong moral compass
- having self-respect, physically and emotionally
- having a sense of humour
- being grateful
- being true to yourself
- honouring your feelings
- being modest, regardless of your situation

Try making a list, even for just one day, of the small ways you might have fulfilled any of these more healthy measures of self-worth. If there's something I've missed here, add to the list for yourself.

For this part to be in any way helpful, you really need to decide on your own values, so off you go with your pen and paper. What do you value in life?

Though we ought not to be in the habit of comparing ourselves to others, you might find it easier to start with the question: What qualities do you value in other people? What do you admire, as opposed to envy? Go deeper than 'the ability to cook a good roast dinner' if you can (though that is a noble value).

Write down your top five values and give this some thought, be lofty in your thinking. When you've done that, write down your own, new definition of success – or at least what you would like it to be. Is it still the outward appearance of success, such as money, nice clothes, etc? Or is success feeling content and being able to sleep soundly at night, comfortable in your own skin (among other things)? Is it about you or is it about how others see you? How are you going to measure how well you are doing? This will be difficult. We all have a slightly warped sense of success, which typically focuses on those external trappings, and as a result, we have a warped sense of our self-worth. But this self-work is worth doing.

Compare the outward yardstick with the inward yardstick – which one do you prefer? Which one do you admire? Which is achievable? Which is sustainable? Which makes you feel good?

Another important note: it's not a case of one or the other. You're not expected to suddenly have no regard for clothing or career achievements, and be at one with nature because material possessions have no real value. That's too extreme. You can still be massively motivated and driven and want to make money (I am) and want to wear nice clothes and appreciate this kind of success, but all of that is a choice. One list of values defines you (e.g. being loyal) and the other (where money is important) is just part of life without taking from or adding to your self-worth. In this sense, you don't need to get the promotion to prove to yourself that you are worthy, you go for the promotion because you want to and you are worthy regardless of the outcome. When this all becomes clear, the next part becomes a whole lot easier.

All of this work enhances your self-esteem and healthy self-esteem enhances your self-confidence, which increases your chances of success, be it the smaller, outer successes that you choose or the bigger, inner successes that define you and that, in turn, maintains your self-esteem. Building self-esteem is essential for achieving real success in your life, so this is where you need to start.

Perfectionism

BEYOND THE SPECIFICS of what we look like or how much money we have in our bank accounts, there is another very broad and hugely significant influence over our sense of self-worth which affects our ability to build on our self-confidence: perfectionism.

Perfectionism is a characteristic that can encompass all of the determinants and domains we've discussed thus far (the perfect relationship, the perfect career, the perfect physique, the perfect reputation, the perfect mood, etc.). However, there are two kinds of perfectionism:

1. Adaptive perfectionism
This kind of perfectionism can, at least on the surface, be seen as a great motivator. Lots of sportspeople, including Serena Williams, think of perfectionism as a blessing, without which they would not have had the same success. For these people, perfectionism is *adaptive*, which is a fancy word for something that helps

you or makes your life easier; it propels them towards their goals. It's not a problem.[30]

2. Maladaptive perfectionism

For others, however, perfectionism can be the mothership measure of self-worth, and the culprit behind so many of our psychological and behavioural issues. When perfectionism becomes a problem, it is, as explained by psychotherapist Mark Tyrrell, referred to as *maladaptive perfectionism*. This kind of perfectionism actually gets in the way of our goals, so this is the kind of perfectionism we really need to avoid.[31]

We cannot talk about or work on our self-confidence without talking about perfectionism – be it adaptive (working for you) or maladaptive (working against you) – and identifying it within ourselves.

If you've been inspired to pick up this book, chances are you sit somewhere on the spectrum between adaptive and maladaptive perfectionism. If perfectionism is not an issue for you in any area of your life, chances are low self-confidence probably isn't an issue either. Likewise, we can't talk about overcoming the fear of failure without exploring this concept.

Again, a large part of this may go back to nurture – how we've been raised and educated in a society in which success is extolled and failure is frowned upon (and even punishable) – while some of it may be driven by nature – your personality.

According to one study carried out at Michigan State University, perfectionist genes may play a bigger role in passing on the personality trait than we would have thought. The researchers examined perfectionism in 146 pairs of identical and fraternal female twins aged twelve to twenty-two. Identical twins, who share 100 per cent of their genetic makeup, scored similarly on tests measuring perfectionism and anxiety. Meanwhile, fraternal twins – who share only 50 per cent of their genetic makeup – recorded less similar scores on measures of perfectionism and anxiety. Lead researcher Jason Moser confirmed that 'there is a significant biological component when it comes to perfectionism that we need to understand more'.[32]

I've come to see maladaptive perfectionism as one of the biggest roadblocks you can come up against, so much so that, even when you *are* successful, it won't feel like success. It can be a motherf*cker of a catch 22. Think about it: if success increases our self-confidence yet we have no real appreciation of success because we immediately think to ourselves, 'well, that was sh*t' or 'that could have been better', we wind up stuck in a perpetual limbo where we crave and pour every ounce of energy into achieving success but can't appreciate it when we get it.

On one hand, you're confident enough to expect the highest standards of yourself, but when such standards remain elusive and permanently out of reach, your self-confidence *can't* increase. What can increase, however, is your fear of failure.

A perfectionist can be simply defined as someone who is unwilling to accept any standard that's short of perfection. Critical self-evaluation tends to come along for the ride, as does concern over how others will evaluate you. In their book *When Perfect Isn't Good Enough: Strategies for Coping with Perfectionism*,[33] Martin Antony and Richard Swinson quote psychiatrist David Burns who, in his 1980 *Psychology Today* piece, said that a perfectionist is someone 'whose standards are high beyond reach or reason'. According to him, this person will 'strain compulsively and unremittingly toward impossible goals and will measure their own worth entirely in terms of productivity and accomplishment'.

Sound familiar? Me too.

While a perfectionist might expect the best from someone else – say, an employee or their own child – this refusal to accept subpar results is, for the most part, focused on themselves. For example, I wouldn't judge another person harshly for not getting the result they wanted or for letting me down, but I expect it from myself and if I don't get it, any compassion that would have easily gone towards someone else goes straight out the window. The kind of perfectionist I would identify with is someone who directs all of their perfectionistic tendencies inwards, becoming their own worst enemy. Their reserves of self-compassion are generally running on empty but they have plenty of compassion for others. Their acceptance of any kind of personal failure is almost non-existent and their connection between maintaining perfection and being worthy is like a live wire – and that is where it's particularly troublesome.

But, as I said, it's not all bad. As characteristics go, perfectionism is definitely a double-edged sword. If you are a perfectionist, you have high standards and when you get going, you work hard until you reach the finish line. (But you're almost never happy with what you've done.) You are passionate and you usually have a very good work ethic (but it might be to your detriment, especially your health's detriment), you have heaps of motivation and determination and you will always go the extra mile. But note, this tends to be only when you're in the midst of something; sometimes you can be so put off by the fear of failing that you don't begin at all. Procrastination can be a constant companion of perfectionists.

You're quick to notice and correct mistakes and, generally, if you're a perfectionist, you'll do quite well (though you may not think you're doing well and you may find fault where it doesn't exist). You also tend to be someone who can be relied upon easily, meaning you'll fare better on your chosen career ladder.

Perfectionism is very necessary within some fields where there can be no room for error. For example, it's important for doctors and medical professionals; it's paramount within science, and for competitive athletes it's absolutely encouraged. While I think of it, perfection is also crucial if you work as an air traffic controller (and I'm sure there are countless other high-stakes jobs where there's less wiggle room for 'well, the plane crashed but you did your best'). But in more subjective and creative realms, and when we're looking at ourselves as a person and not what we do, perfectionism can drive us up the wall. If there's no clear right or wrong, how can you ever measure if something is good enough or as good as it can be? And if it's all about how you appear but not about how you feel (i.e. you appear successful to others and you've got the most enviable LinkedIn profile of all, but you feel like sh*t on the inside), is it really serving you all that well?

Perfectionism can be found in some or all of the following domains, as laid out by psychologist and co-author of *When Perfect Isn't Good Enough*, Martin Antony:[34]

- performance at work or school – this is the biggest one for me and, I imagine, for most people because this is always where we've been consistently and systematically evaluated
- relationships, friends and family life
- leisure and recreation – some perfectionist will give no time whatsoever to leisure because they are so focused on work
- neatness, cleanliness and aesthetics
- organisation and ordering – not really a problem for me, connoisseur of the 'floordrobe' that I am
- communication (e.g. writing, speaking)
- physical appearance – another biggie
- health (e.g. diet and exercise).

Perfectionism in some of these areas in small amounts can be helpful. Maladaptive perfectionism is experienced when things get a little too extreme, branching out into multiple areas or domains of life and really taking over.

The thing is, it can go far beyond carrying out a task or performing in the outside world, it can encompass every aspect of your inner world. In this sense, we don't just expect perfect results out there, we expect ourselves to be perfect in every way: the perfect friend, the perfect child, the perfect sibling, the perfect girlfriend, the perfect work colleague, the perfect sleeper, the perfect partner in the sack, the perfect host – the list goes on. We might not even tolerate imperfection in our thoughts (which might explain why I've found meditation so bloody hard).

To some people it might seem like an admirable trait – I used to see it as a badge of honour that meant I was incredibly conscientious – but for those of us who are plagued with perfectionist thinking, it can be more of a psychological handicap, more self-defeating than self-motivating.

How does it affect me? If I felt anxious in the past, I'd get upset and angry with myself. Although I didn't consciously draw this conclusion, my anxious tendencies were proof to me that I was not perfect. If I act irrationally out of emotion towards my family or my partner, I get frustrated that my emotions aren't perfectly balanced. If I catch a glimpse of cellulite on my thighs – by the way, remind me to punch the person who ever pointed out that cellulite was a bad thing when almost every woman I know has it and it's so very normal – I say to myself, 'I need to work on that and get rid of it.' But there is another part to that sentence that goes like this: 'So that it will be perfect, so that I will be confident.' I even get frustrated with myself if I catch a flu, which is hardly within my control, because it means my health isn't perfect. And because I expect the best, I am allergic to getting it wrong. If it's not perfect, it means I'm not good enough – but it shouldn't be like that.

Expecting yourself to be perfect is the most futile thing of all, and one thing's for sure, it's exhausting. If you're a maladaptive perfectionist, you're a hamster on a wheel, always striving for 100 per cent perfection – and accepting no less – so that you can finally feel confident and validated. You may as well wait for Godot to arrive. (Spoiler: he never does.)

Why is it that a perfectionist can't feel confident when they've done a good job on something? Because there's always something they could have done better – a level of perfection that cannot be reached.

Though it might sometimes sound like a perfectionist has a high opinion of themselves, it does not mean they think they are amazing or exceptionally talented – quite the opposite, in fact. It means you expect yourself to perform faultlessly and be the best you can be within yourself and what's important to you. Perfectionists are very hard on themselves and find it very hard to see the small victories or discover the partial successes in anything.

You have to ask the following questions of your perfectionist tendencies: if everything must be perfect, can anything ever be good enough? And if nothing can ever be good enough, because total perfection is unrealistic in most parts of our lives, can we enjoy anything at all? If success itself is laden with self-criticism ('I did it but it could have been better'), is it worth aspiring to in the first place? Yes, you might have got the promotion and you might be able to flash the cash, but is your day-to-day experience of life the better for it? Are you so concerned about getting it right that all you wind up dwelling on are the circumstances where you've got it wrong?

Not sure if you're a perfectionist? Here are some indicators of maladaptive perfectionism. They might sound dramatic but they're very easy habits to slip into (I certainly do):

- o inflexible, impossibly high standards
- o having an all-or-nothing approach, black-and-white thinking, right or wrong – there's no in between
- o procrastinating
- o 'should' self-talk ('I should have done better')
- o highly self-critical
- o highly sensitive to criticism from others because that would question your perfectionism
- o focusing entirely on the end result
- o seeing no value in partial success
- o having little value in leisure because 'what's the point?'
- o finding fault with your work that others can't see

- thinking mistakes are a sign of personal defects
- not able to take a compliment, self-deprecating
- seeing success as the goal, but it never being enough
- feeling down and really bad about yourself if something doesn't go to plan
- having a skewed view – skewed towards the negative – about how things went
- having a strong fear of imperfection and failure
- overestimating the likelihood of negative events
- underestimating your ability to cope with negative events
- having a strong need to be in control and aversion to uncertainty

Do you recognise any of the above in yourself? As always, this is just for you, so be honest. If any of the above sound familiar, your confidence is in jeopardy.

Psychologist and co-author of *When Perfect Isn't Good Enough* Martin Antony asks the following questions of his clients and patients, when he is determining whether or not their standards are overly perfectionistic (pen and paper time):

1 Are my standards higher than those of other people?
2 Am I able to meet my standards?
3 Do I get upset if I don't meet my standards?
4 Do my standards help me to achieve my goal or do they get in the way?

5 What would be the costs and benefits of relaxing a standard or ignoring a rule?

Loosening the shackles of perfectionism – both perfection-istic thinking and perfectionistic behaviour – is not easy. It's one of the big challenges you can take on but loosen them you must in order to improve your confidence.

If you can dial it down (as opposed to trying to remove all perfectionist tendencies from your mind), life gets a whole lot more interesting and enjoyable. Failure becomes more tolerable and inconsistencies add to the rich tapestry of life. You start to explore the grey areas rather than living entirely in black and white, ruled by an all-or-nothing existence. You reduce the fear of failure because you learn that there is such a thing as 'good enough' and not being perfect or not getting a perfect result doesn't affect your sense of self-worth. It's not that you throw all your motivation in the bin, but you stop being your harshest critic.

You become far more forgiving of yourself. But while I know this, I'm no expert and I've really struggled to keep myself from resorting back to maladaptive thinking.

You might learn to be kinder and more tolerant about the fact that you are human, but for me, perfectionist thinking can creep back if I don't check in from time to time, especially when the chips are down. What I mean here is it's always much easier to be kind to yourself when things are going well and as soon as things take a turn for the worse, along comes that inner maladaptive bitch.

Until very recently, I didn't understand quite how much it could seep into every area of my life and stop me from enjoying and feeling good about myself, and actually bring about stress and anxiety. When I stopped for a moment and observed the ways in which I might actually show all the signs of an unhealthy perfectionist, it became clear just how much it was fuelling my fear of failure and inhibiting my self-confidence. It became clear that, as a perfectionist, I might always be plagued with self-doubt. I'll give you an example.

With my first book, I was even more clueless and unsure than I am now – and, with my first few chapters, I poured my heart and soul into it, aiming for perfection, whatever the hell that was. I would then send a chapter or two to my (very encouraging) editor and, as a busy publishing director, she might not reply within five minutes. Someone who isn't a perfectionist would carry on with the rest of their tasks. For me, however, in between sending it and receiving feedback, my mind went straight to, 'Oh, she must have read it and thinks it's awful and doesn't know how to say it to me. Maybe they're regretting going ahead with this book at all.'

I started to question everything. I would also send those initial emails along with messages like 'Okay this is *not* properly edited yet and it's probably sh*t' or 'Oh God, I have no idea what I'm doing', so that I could defend myself if it wasn't perfect, before anyone else had a chance to say anything. The next day I'd hear back, as I always would, and to my complete surprise I was told that it was fantastic and that I was definitely on the right track. I would be happy and relieved, yes, but also a bit frustrated with myself for letting the self-doubt consume me like a fire.

To me, if it wasn't perfect from the get-go, I was doomed. I wouldn't allow myself the room for learning or figuring things out or the fact that I'd never done this before. Had my editor said, 'It's okay but it needs work', I know from previous experience that I would probably have cried, but, worse than this, the belief that I'm not good enough could have lodged itself as a permanent fixture in my brain. Naturally enough, this constant yearning for perfection became something pretty enormous that (a) wrecked my buzz and (b) I wanted to work on.

Nine ways to challenge perfectionist thinking

The thought of undoing such an enormously ingrained pattern of thinking and behaviour is stressful in itself. But, remember, it's merely a mindset that can be altered with small amounts of regular effort and patience. This part's really important: the perfectionist part of your brain doesn't need to be lopped off entirely, it just needs to be softened a little. I don't want to ignore my perfectionism entirely because with it, I am passionate about what I do. I like that I give my best to whatever I take on, but my best could, at least sometimes, be enough.

1. Patience

For starters, don't expect to alter your thinking about perfectionism overnight. If you're getting frustrated at yourself because you find yourself slipping back into perfectionist thinking, that's just your maladaptive perfectionism at work (ironically).

Decide which kind of perfectionism you are going to allow: adaptive, which is healthy and serves you well; or maladaptive, which can be downright neurotic and suck the joy right out of your life. A healthy perfectionist will still be motivated by high standards, but their ideal outcome will be something to aim for, as opposed to an absolute all-or-nothing goal, where anything short of it equals failure (of both the task and you as a person).

For a healthy perfectionist, failure won't necessarily be celebrated – let's not expect miracles – but it won't pin them down like a gigantic paperweight. It won't define them.

2. Cognitive restructuring

This sounds fancy but it's simply about putting your thoughts and your beliefs on trial. The task is to examine regularly the evidence that supports or rubbishes your perfectionistic thinking surrounding a particular thing and to look objectively at the facts. Are you less of a person if you don't get the highest grade possible? Am I really a bad writer if this book flops? Does not getting it right really mean I'm not good enough or will never be good enough? Cross-examine your thoughts and feelings with the reality of the situation you're in. Look to the past for confirmation. When you realise that a particular thought is not based on any truth, write down a new, more realistic alternative.

3. Adjusting standards

Overcoming perfectionism is essentially about reframing your standards, where possible, so that they are reachable with effort and determined by you (not someone else). If you are the one to set your own standards, yet you can never measure up to them, something's not quite right. Shouldn't we set our own standards to suit ourselves? In my experience, if you set unrealistic and unreachable goals and you fail to achieve them, you experience a strong sense of failure, coupled with low self-esteem and high self-blame.

It's wonderful to achieve beyond what you'd expected from time to time, but it's just not realistic to sustain that on an ongoing basis, and true perfectionists tend to aspire to heights that simply don't exist. Set a standard for yourself with your next task that you would be approving of and encouraging of if you were setting the standard for someone else you care about. Set a standard that is still high but achievable. If you set a standard that is impossibly high, and that can never be reached, you have to understand that you may feel down, and you may never feel accomplished. At the same time, there may be standards that you want to keep, such as in your career, but you might recognise that perfectionism is a problem in your personal life so maybe there is some room for adjusting of standards there.

4. Perspective shifting

A healthy approach to perfectionism surrounding a particular issue is to take out a pen and paper and write down what you would say to a friend who is in the same position and endlessly critical of themselves. This is a version of social comparison that can be helpful. It enables us to examine the evidence objectively without emotion by taking ourselves out of the equation. What would you say to someone who failed? Would you tell them they're clearly just not good enough? If you spoke to that friend the way you speak to yourself, they probably wouldn't want to keep you around. They might even call you a dick.

Here you can also examine and challenge your double standards: why have a more lenient set of standards for someone else but impose a harsher set of rules for yourself? Corny as it sounds, we really need to befriend ourselves. Why are we so understanding of and kind to others and so bloody brutal when it comes to the most important person of all? Maybe your perfectionistic thinking was first brought on by pressuring parents, but as an adult, the pressure to be perfect in all of these ways comes from you alone (I understand that a certain amount of pressure to perform at work will come from your boss, but I'm talking about the pressure from you alone to be perfect in every way as a human being). If we go out of our way to avoid people who give us an unnecessary hard time in life, why do we put up with it when it's coming from ourselves?

5. Good doesn't have to mean perfect

As Henry James put it, 'Excellence does not require perfection.' Remind yourself that something really great doesn't need to be flawless. Even excellence is a pretty lofty goal; instead, the greatest aim we can have is to do the best that we can. As a healthy perfectionist, you can strive for greatness without compromising your self-esteem, while at the same time you can derive pleasure from your efforts along the way. This is what I'm choosing.

6. Rethinking perfectionism

Also, the thing I try to remind myself about perfection is that if it's constant, it's really f*cking boring. Think about someone you adore. Do you adore them because they are flawless and perfect or do you find their quirks and idiosyncrasies and 'flaws' endearing? If I don't have a bit of a bicker with my fiancé every now and then, I don't fully appreciate the other 95 per cent of times that are good. If every day is the perfect day, do they not all become very normal and ordinary and vanilla flavoured?

For me, perfection is a psychological construct we mistakenly strive for, but let me tell you, it's not a reality. It helps to go back to your core values and beliefs about yourself (which we explored in Chapter 5) and make adjustments so that they are fair, realistic and not destructive.

7. Behavioural experiments

Another thing to do here is to actively seek out opportunities where you can make mistakes and live with it – the point is in how you respond to the 'failure'. Will the world fall apart? No. If you actually make imperfection or failure the goal with things that don't carry as much weight for you, you can lessen the impact of getting it wrong – or less than 100 per cent perfection – when it comes to something that is important. You can learn to tolerate and be okay with 'good enough' and, as a result, develop more flexible thinking.

Being able to say, 'Yeah, I got it wrong, and that's okay' or 'I made a mistake, I'm only human', softens your straight line thinking – which can be tough going – and allows for a little more of that much-needed self-compassion. Experiment with actions where the consequences of making a mistake are minimal and try to get comfortable with it.

8. Encourage a wider context

Psychotherapist Mark Tyrrell recommends this one. 'Chronic perfectionists consider experiences in too narrow a context, and so they may miss the wider contexts of what and why they were doing something.'[35] Practise bigger picture thinking. For example, instead of seeing the goal being achieved as the point of it all, what if you see it as an opportunity to be creatively stretched, regardless of the outcome?

9. Encourage downtime

This one's so important. Do you know someone who is so goal-focused that they don't really get any enjoyment out of downtime? Tyrrell explains that, for some perfectionists, life can feel pretty meaningless unless it's always results-driven. Free time doing something that serves no purpose other than to be enjoyable is rarely valued in what he describes as a 'repressive psychological regime'.[36]

Start to prioritise downtime as not just something in between your normal results-oriented routine but something to be valued and appreciated.

Imposter Syndrome & the Confidence Gap between Men and Women

IT WOULD SEEM that something was missing if I wrote a book about confidence in the twenty-first century and skipped over the topic that you'll find emblazoned on the cover of many women's interest magazines for the past twenty-four months: imposter syndrome. It would also be foolish to overlook the confidence gap that exists between men and women, which directly relates to imposter syndrome.

Technically speaking, imposter syndrome is merely a trendy and sensationalised title given to something that people have experienced for generations: the fear of not being good enough and the fear that, someday soon, our inadequacy will become known to all. It's essentially a disconnect between our public and private self-concepts. It's a feeling that what we put out there is at odds with how we see ourselves privately. I don't know about you, but I'm still waiting for the fraud police to knock on my door any minute now.

In today's label-loving world, imposter syndrome is yet another fairly normal aspect of the human experience that's been boxed off as a rather sinister psychological condition, and something else for us to worry over and obsess about curing.

For starters, I'm not sure I entirely agree with the severity of labelling things as syndromes and conditions, especially when you're self-diagnosing, because perhaps that's just more beating yourself up for not being perfect. Do we really need, at this point, to be harder on ourselves than we already are? After all, imposter syndrome doesn't technically fit the clinical criteria for a psychological syndrome, which refers to intense symptoms that get in the way of our normal functioning. So let's not think of it as a mental illness; it's just something we experience. It can be moderate for some and more acute for others.

Whatever you decide to call it – a syndrome, a phenomenon, a pain in the arse – it's something we can relate to, especially those among us who are high-achieving, and it's something that can get in the way of pursuing our goals.

While it would be incorrect to describe it as a female-only issue, recent research has certainly highlighted it as something that affects a lot more women than men, or at least has more of an impact on women. A recent study by career developments agency Amazing If[37] showed that 40 per cent of millennial women (taken to mean women born between 1980 and the mid-1990s) felt intimidated by senior people at work, when compared with just 22 per cent of men. One third of the women asked reported strong feelings of self-doubt at work while 63 per cent of women believed that their imposter syndrome would affect their chances of success.

Apart from fearing that we're not good enough, when we do experience success, we feel as though we're undeserving of it. Imposter syndrome usually refers to our own judgement about ourselves in a work situation, but, generally speaking, it relates to a default setting of self-doubt. Is what I've achieved good enough? Am I good enough to do it? Do I deserve this opportunity? Do I deserve my success? Is my being in this position a fluke? Will people think I am a fraud? Asking yourself these kinds of questions – which I've asked myself throughout my career – is the hallmark of an imposter mindset.

A true imposter, though, is someone posing as something or someone they are not. If I talked my way into a job as a chef in a Michelin-star restaurant and got lucky on my first night when baked beans and toast was on the menu, then my self-doubt would be rational and based on the evidence and facts (that I, admittedly, have elementary-level cooking skills). So why, when I've been writing for the past ten years, do I feel like a fraud of the same level? Why do I think I am fooling people? This kind of self-doubt still invades our thinking despite the often overwhelming evidence to the contrary. Why is this? Well, there might be a few reasons why you might be experiencing imposter syndrome:

1 Like perfectionism and our fear of failure, imposter syndrome can stem from certain family dynamics and how we were reared or taught in school. Maybe you have a sibling who was designated as the intelligent, book-smart member of the family. Maybe you couldn't live up to that standard. Maybe, on the other hand, you've been told how perfect you are all your life and how you could achieve anything you wanted to, and when you finally went out into the real world and realised that failure was going to present itself at some point, you began to doubt yourself.

2 Sometimes, it's because what you are working on doesn't directly relate to what you've studied or trained in during your education. We feel we don't have the skills - on paper - therefore we must be

inadequate, despite the fact that so many important roles are not determined by the subjects a person took at school. A car mechanic, who trained specifically for their career and got the piece of paper to prove it, might not doubt themselves, whereas a writer or a poet might suffer doubts because what they are doing is less tangible. In certain roles, we may have just as much experience, but no certificate to validate it.

3 Sometimes, it's because we rely heavily on social comparison, looking at how other people are doing in work or how people appear to be doing on social media, with a warped perception that we are always on the back foot. For me, and all other writers out there, there's no bigger vehicle for comparison than the bestseller list. As we've already discussed, it's very easy to create the picture of success on Instagram. People share their highlights but rarely the moments when they've been sh*tting bricks about something. We need to stop comparing our behind-the-scenes with someone else's highlights reel. The former is fuelled by self-doubt and not necessarily true, while the latter is curated beyond reality. It's crucial to remember that we're living inside our own heads – as obvious as that sounds. We can hear all the negativity and self-doubt chatter telling us that we are yet again flying by the seat of our pants, but we can't hear it from other people's heads, unless they talk about

it. Therefore, they appear confident and competent and we decide that this must be the truth, but we don't see their own self-doubt that accompanies it.

4 Sometimes, it comes about because of your environment, such as if you work in a highly competitive field with lots of showboating and pissing contests (or whatever the female equivalent of that might be). Society, you might argue, has grown to foster showboating, especially with social media. You'll see this demonstrated in all of those quantitative 'top tens', 'best dressed', 'going up/ going down' lists. While this is commonplace in society, all you control is whether or not you are happy with what you've achieved.

5 Other times, it goes hand in hand with a lack of experience, which is why it's so common among those aged eighteen to thirty-four who are only finding their feet in their careers. In creative roles, there is no such rinse and repeat formula that we can learn, practise and do again until we feel absolutely sure of our ability. For me, every project is different and each new job flexes a new muscle within me creatively; while I might get one thing done and feel I have it nailed, a new challenge will come my way and I'm straight back to, 'Oh sh*t, I have no idea what I'm doing.' I literally feel it every time I sit down to work.

6 For women, though, our experience of imposter syndrome may derive from the deeply ingrained

sexist stereotyping which has meant that women have, collectively, been more scrutinised in the workplace and have had to work harder to prove themselves and to earn more money than their male counterpart. It's not necessarily something we're all conscious of, but it's there, deep in our cultural conditioning.

Pauline Rose Clance and Suzanne Imes in their 1970s paper 'The Impostor Phenomenon in High Achieving Women' explain that for women, success is 'contraindicated by societal expectations and their own internalized self-evaluations'.[38] In other words, we are dealing with internalised narratives about our perceived lack of qualifications: 'Despite outstanding academic and professional accomplishments, women who experience the impostor phenomenon persist in believing that they are really not bright and have fooled anyone who thinks otherwise.'

Why might this be? We can blame history in part. For so long, the majority of professional roles were filled by men. This was the way of the world and it set in motion a conditioning that pervaded the psyche of both men and women for generations. For starters, it wasn't until 1922 that all Irish women over the age of twenty-one were allowed to vote, something that only followed a long, arduous campaign led by women. Italian women had to wait until 1945. During the Second World War, American women had the opportunity to work in traditional male roles when huge numbers of men left for war. However, when the war was over, men resumed these roles and a lot of women were pushed back to secretarial roles which, at the time, were deemed more 'feminine', or were just pushed out of the workforce entirely.

It really wasn't until the 1960s – helped by feminist movements around the world – that women began to enter the workforce in great numbers and not just because men were busy doing something else. It was unusual then to see a woman in a man's role, and to this day, in some professions, we're still – at least subconsciously – getting used to the idea. After all, in the grand scheme of things, the 1960s really weren't that long ago. What's more, it wasn't until the 1970s that the UK enacted their Equal Pay Act, which prohibited any less favourable treatment between men and women in the workplace. It also wasn't until 1973 that women in Ireland were allowed to keep their jobs (in the civil service and many private companies) after they were married. Up to then they were forced to give them up, due to the marriage bar, which had been in place since 1932. My own grandmother came first in the entire country in the civil service state exams. Despite her clear ability, when she married, she was forced to resign and assume life as her husband's 'chattel' (in much the same way you might own a purebred cow). Infuriating, isn't it?

In many ways, we've come a long way since my nana and other women had to deal with that kind of sh*t, but if you look at contemporary Hollywood as just one example, it's clear that while women may appear to have equal opportunities, the gender pay gap, for one thing, still very much exists. Though we might not want to admit it, sexism still pervades many a workplace. As Sheryl Sandberg points out in *Lean In*, it's still a man's world.[39] When she published her book in March 2013, she cited that only twenty-one companies out of the top 500 by revenue were headed up by women, while American women earned seventy-seven cents to every dollar earned by a man.

Because of all of this (and there is so much more than my word count will allow for), it's long been said that a woman has to work twice as hard to be taken half as seriously as a man, and is still the case today. Is it surprising at all that women struggle with confidence and are more vulnerable to imposter syndrome when you consider all that history and cultural context? To this day, we may still be comparing ourselves and our competence to the stereotypical fit for the role in question: a man.

Whether it's a cultural or biological issue, we also know that women are more likely to blame themselves for a perceived failure or a setback. We're inclined to internalise everything, whereas men might blame something else. Women, it's acknowledged, are more likely to have lower expectations than men when it comes to their performance across a wide variety of tasks. Again, this may come back to insecurities about proving ourselves on a level playing field with men. As Katty Kay, the Washington DC anchor for BBC World News America, and Claire Shipman, an ABC News and *Good Morning America* correspondent, state in their book *The Confidence Code*, women will tend to think there's someone who could do a better job – possibly because it would have formerly been a role for a man – and struggle to accept praise and professional validation.[40]

What's more, Pauline Rose Clance and Suzanne Imes found, women look for explanations for their accomplishments beyond their own intelligence. An unexpected performance outcome will be attributed to a temporary cause, such as luck, whereas men 'own success as attributable to a quality inherent in themselves: ability'.[41]

For women, imposter syndrome may have deep roots in gender issues but let's be clear: men are not immune. Imposter syndrome is not entirely non-existent for men – in fact, some research says they feel it just as much but their reasons for feeling it may be more about inexperience, and pressure to achieve from other sources rather than comparing themselves to the perceived competencies of the opposite sex.

In the 1990s, Clance and Imes made some amendments to their 1970s paper, explaining that, in their more recent research, some men reported feeling like an imposter but they were just less likely to speak about it openly. The reason for this, Clance and Imes explain, may be because men feel under pressure to conform to the stereotype that portrays them as confident and not appearing insecure. Men, they surmised, would fear a backlash if they were to speak openly about their imposter syndrome.[42]

Is there anything you can do about it?

If you've felt like a cheap brand of bubbly posing as a bottle of Bollinger, you're not alone. With 70 per cent of people being said to have experienced it, according to a study in the *International Journal of Behavioural Science*, it's now referred to as 'workplace anxiety du jour' (Slate.com).[43]

It's also not just something we experience in our twenties and thirties. Maya Angelou, the Pulitzer-prize-nominated American poet, was much quoted for stating, 'I have written eleven books, but each time I think, "Uh oh, they're going to find out now. I've run a game on everybody, and they're going to find me out."' Likewise, Meryl Streep fessed up that she has been plagued with self-doubt, saying, 'I don't know how to act anyway, so why am I doing this?' In spite of the fact that she's been nominated for more Oscars than any other actor. If she played the same role over and over again, she'd probably feel sure that she has it down to a fine art, but like so many of us, there's a different challenge each time (which is also what we want and what keeps us interested and motivated; this feeling of imposter syndrome is merely an unwanted side-effect, unfortunately). If Meryl and Maya struggled to accept the evidence, then we shouldn't be too hard on ourselves for this default behaviour either.

But we can work on our fraudulent feelings so they no longer get in the way of success. Here are four things to remember:

1 First and foremost, it's not about experiencing a string of successes, so don't go putting additional pressure on yourself here. In fact, Clance and Imes' research found that repeated successes were not enough to break the self-perpetuating nature of imposter syndrome.

2 Instead, we need to get straight back to cognitive restructuring, which is all about putting your thoughts on trial and cross-examining them against the evidence. Are you really fooling people? Are the people you are fooling really so incompetent that they couldn't tell if you, yourself, were entirely incompetent?

3 Then, we must prioritise and give more weight and respect to our transferable skills. I've always felt

that my bachelor's degree and my master's were so vague – Communication Studies and an MA in Film and Television Studies – that I am sometimes afraid to say I have them, in case someone were to ask me a question based on what I should have learned about. I put them down as nothing more than years spent thinking about what I might like to do when in reality, I definitely came away with skills that I am now applying on a daily basis.

If I want to be a professional juggler I need to develop my skills as a juggler, plain and simple. But if I want to work with people in a communications role, my social and interpersonal skills and my ability to think critically and creatively are among the wider, more general skills that will lend themselves to countless jobs. These aren't just skills you gain in education; most of the time, we do the real learning through experience in work. We need to stop being obsessed with the idea of having everything bullet-pointed on paper, which stems from our school days when that's how success and ability was measured. How you problem-solve, how you manage situations and the fact that you think innovatively are just as important as the finer details.

4 On the gender issue, we need to stop assuming that men are automatically more competent and better than women. Confidence matters more than competence, when it comes to imposter syndrome.

You are not less skilled or less capable than someone else, you just have more self-doubt, which you can work on, while the rest of the world works on the bigger task at hand: bridging the gap between men and women.

In saying all of this, imposter syndrome isn't all bad and we shouldn't try to stamp it out entirely, provided it's not interfering with our actions too much. We can, instead, work on our perception of imposter syndrome and turn it around so it works for us rather than against us. You can choose to own it.

Why?

Because ...

1 If you don't have a breeze about what you are doing, you are in good company. If you know exactly what you are doing at all times, you're not taking any risks, which means you won't make mistakes from which you learn and develop confidence.
2 If you feel as though you're on shaky ground, you're challenging yourself and testing the boundaries of your comfort zone.
3 Sometimes, it's better to underestimate your abilities than to overestimate them, as this means you'll be neither disappointed nor overly confident.

4 People with high imposter-minded tendencies tend to have a strong sense of humility, which is an affable trait.

5 Remember, it's the flipside to a personality that is driven to experience new things and self-improve. I am motivated by personal development, which means I will always be trying something new. More than someone who is happy in their comfort zone, I'm going to feel uneasy and unsure of what I'm doing.

6 It's incredibly normal to feel like you don't belong outside of your comfort zone, but remember, this is the learning zone and good things can happen here.

7 If someone has never felt like a fraud, not ever, they're probably the one who's the most incompetent.

8 If you possess the self-awareness to be able to think that you might be a fraud, you're probably not one. It's like worrying about going insane. Remember, those who are truly incompetent (or insane) rarely spend time worrying about it. This is the proven Dunning-Kruger effect, discovered in 1999 when Justin Kruger and David Dunning from Cornell University tested whether people who lack the skills or abilities for something are also more likely to lack awareness of their lack of ability. They tested people's ability to analyse their own abilities by setting tests, such as logical reasoning and grammar. Their tests found that those people who performed the worst were also the worst at estimating their own aptitude.[44] So you're probably grand.

What else can you do about your fraudulent feelings?

1 Observe the thoughts and feelings, allow for them but don't assume you have to obey them. Act in accordance with logic and reason and, if you're in doubt, examine the supporting evidence.
2 Accept that, like anxiety, it's a very normal human experience, but don't let it dictate your actions.
3 Talk openly about your feelings with a manager or someone you trust.
4 Take comfort in the fact that you're not the only person who feels this way. Think of Meryl Streep.

Exercise:
ACCEPTING COMPLIMENTS

One of the best ways to start challenging your self-perpetuating imposterism is to work on your ability to accept positive feedback. If you struggle with imposter syndrome, you definitely struggle with compliments. So when, for instance, someone says to me, 'We really appreciate your work on this; you've done a great job', I should not be so quick to say, 'Well, it was nothing at all.' I could say, 'Thank you, that's good to hear.'
The next time you are told something nice about your work, you need to listen, take it in and get as much

nourishment from the positive feedback on your competence as you can. It helps to keep a record of the feedback you receive. Be mindful of the trap where you take positive feedback on one thing to mean you disappointed people on other things. Take it at face value and don't look for hidden meanings. You don't have to say, 'I know, I'm great', but you can be gracious, warm and receptive.

There has been heaps of research carried out on the confidence gap between men and women - I really recommend reading *The Confidence Gap* by Russ Harris, *The Confidence Code* by Katty Kay and Claire Shipman and, of course, Sheryl Sandberg's book, to get you started.

PART TWO

THE TOOLKIT

Tool #1 – Stoicism And Why It's The Sh*t

'Make the best use of what is in your power and take the rest as it happens. Some things are up to us and some things are not up to us.'

Epictetus

STOICISM IS the new avocado and tool number one. It's made up of several smaller tools within your confidence kit that should be returned to again and again and again (and, yes, *again*).

First, a little history lesson. Stoicism is a branch of Ancient Greek philosophy founded in the third century BC. Its three primary leaders were Marcus Aurelius, Seneca and Epictetus. Definitions on stoicism are long and varied, for example dictionary.com refers to it as 'indifference to pleasure or pain', while Google dictionary describes it as a school which taught that virtue and the highest good is based on knowledge; the wise live in harmony with the divine Reason (also identified with Fate and Providence) that governs nature, and are indifferent to the vicissitudes of fortune and to pleasure and pain.

Bit too hifalutin?

In layman's terms, it's a school of thought that's heavily rooted in logic and reason. It can be defined as a human path to happiness, found in accepting the present moment as it presents itself and not allowing ourselves to be controlled by our desire for pleasure or our fear of pain, by using our minds to understand the world around us and to do our part in nature's plan, and by working together and treating others in a fair and just manner.

Stoicism doesn't just work wonders when it comes to confidence and managing your fears surrounding failure, it can enhance every single aspect of your life, making every decision and challenge that bit easier to navigate (however, don't expect to skim through this chapter and have nailed the art of stoicism; it takes a little bit of conscious effort on a daily basis before your grey matter gets it).

Though stoicism is heavily linked with historical icons such as Marcus Aurelius, fans of stoicism would advocate that there is a stoic within every one of us. With a little coaxing – and maturity – it's only in recent years that mine has started to wake up.

Now, if you go digging into stoicism, you might be put off at first. I was. You'll find that a lot of the early texts are written in very flowery language, referring to gods and higher powers and living in accordance with nature and cardinal virtues, some of which can send your bullsh*tometer into orbit. On the surface, it might sound a bit airy-fairy, but the most important parts, which we'll tease out here, are actually not very complicated, they're grounded in reality and are refreshingly logical. In recent years, stoicism has resurfaced in popular psychology – author and renowned podcaster Tim Ferriss is one of its most notable contemporary advocates – and has been reconsidered with our modern way of life in mind. The reason for its resurgence, I'm guessing, is that we're more anxious than ever before (the number of searches with 'anxiety' have doubled in the past five years, according to Google Trends), so we're turning to the wise ones of days gone by to steer us in the right direction.

In this chapter, I will offer my take on stoicism, the principles worth reminding yourself of on a daily basis and precisely how they might apply to an increased sense of self-confidence.

For me, stoicism is a tool that helps to direct and guide my actions (and, to a certain extent, my thoughts) so that I can remain calm and rational in what is a very unpredictable world. Instead of controlling what happens to us, which we try so hard to do with little success, we control how we react to what happens to us.

The principles of stoicism can help to illuminate what's good and what's bad, what matters in life and what doesn't. Stoicism is all about logical thought and one of its central concepts is that your feelings come from your thoughts. Epictetus said, 'It isn't events themselves that disturb people, but only their judgements about them.' The weather didn't ruin your wedding day, your being pissed off about it did.

My favourite stoic principles are as follows.

1. Accept what you can't control
Among the many teachings within stoicism – some of which might seem a bit waffly – this is the principle that matters most to me: accepting that which you cannot control and focusing your energy on that which you can. It's about distinguishing between what is up to us and what is not, as Epictetus says so eloquently in the quotation at the start of this chapter, and then acting accordingly.

This sounds easy, but it's not. It requires a calm rationality that sometimes feels impossible to maintain when our emotions run amok and we get caught up in the minutiae of everyday life. When you're absolutely fuming about some unfathomable injustice, such as an asshole who has cut in front of you in traffic without indicating and you're momentarily praying for a plague of locusts to invade their home, your inner stoic can be hard to muster. Similarly, if you're overlooked for a promotion in work, it may not be because you weren't good enough, and you will have to dig deep to come to terms with the reality (which is something you cannot control). So often, and without even realising, we push against these immovable objects, which are things we cannot control or predict, hoping to change things. And when we don't succeed, we become stressed, knackered, frustrated, angry and anxious; we experience some or all of those crappy feelings, depending on the circumstances, that we're trying so hard to keep at bay. Well, it doesn't have to be that way if you don't want it to be.

In stoicism, the things we cannot control are considered external events and, as far as I'm concerned, it's external events that challenge our self-confidence. External events are unpredictable, such as someone cutting across us in a meeting, someone else's reaction to us, whether or not the microphone will break down when you're giving a presentation, and so on and so forth. We shouldn't try to control external events and, while we're at it, we shouldn't rely on them for our happiness (such as depending on your career credentials alone for a feeling of contentment).

What we can do (with practice) is control ourselves and our reactions to such external events and rely on ourselves (e.g. setting a good morning routine) to dictate our mood on a daily basis. We can control how we prepare ourselves ahead of a challenge, for example, even though we cannot fully control the outcome. Stoicism, in this sense, requires a lot of what we're taught in Disney's *Frozen*: 'Let it go'. Or as I prefer: 'Let that sh*t go', because, for some reason, curse words seem to pack a more powerful punch for me. Let go of what you can't control and concern yourself only with what you can.

I'll give you an example that presented itself to me as a unique behavioural experiment in the art of stoicism. A few years ago, a male friend got back into a relationship that, at first, I was not at all in favour of. The girl hadn't treated him well in the past and I was concerned that he would be hurt again and deserved better. I wasn't happy about it and he knew this, but he also understood why I felt this way and allowed for it (he clearly had this stoicism thing nailed). I selfishly hoped I could make him see things from my perspective. I wanted to change something I couldn't control – his actions and his feelings.

On the contrary, he didn't feel the need to change what he couldn't control, which was other people's reactions to his rekindled romance. He focused his energy instead on what he could control – how he himself felt about it and what was best for him – because it was pointless worrying about what other people might think when, really, he was the only one who was affected. They got back together (still are!) and he was very happy, so much happier than he had been before.

I realised very quickly that hurling myself at this immovable object would not only be a waste of energy but would also affect my mood and potentially my friendship. I didn't like feeling selfish and frustrated; they're hardly the most likeable of attributes. I was scared that their getting back together would drive a wedge between me and my friend. But then, as I was trying to wrap my head around my thinking, I realised that *this* was something I could control. If I didn't want there to be a wedge, I didn't have to put it there. If I wanted my friend to be happy, I could let him be. I couldn't see into the future and control whether or not this relationship would serve him well. I had to let it go and be there for him, regardless of the outcome. I could, with a little effort, control my reaction to this change, instead of trying to control the change itself. I could allow myself to feel those negatives and then rationalise my thoughts and feelings which would directly impact on my behaviour towards my friend. I could breathe for a moment before acting. It's not that I was acting one way while feeling another; when I allowed a moment (okay, several moments) for logic and reason, it changed my feelings about it, which then steered my behaviour.

This is stoicism at work – choosing to act on what can be acted on. So often, we think of our thoughts and emotions as things that just happen to us, that we have no control over, but if you make an effort, how they affect you *can* become a choice.

There is a space between your emotions and your actions. Step into it.

As explained by Ryan Holiday in *The Daily Stoic*, which is a valuable online resource and a seminal book with a daily message that I keep beside my bed, the original stoics (Seneca and the lads) believed that the source of our dissatisfaction lay in our impulsive dependency on our reflexive senses (my emotion-fuelled reaction above, for example), rather than logic (what prevailed when I looked at the facts of what can and cannot be controlled).[45]

The lesson?

Take a moment. Think before you act. If something is outside of your control, and you try to change it but can't, you'll feel like pants. The above scenario was not up to me and, therefore, not my concern or my business. So I had to redirect my energy towards what was up to me if I wanted to feel better about things. Here's a reminder of what you can and cannot control. It's very simple really.

Up to you / worthy of control and energy:

o Your actions: Preparation for a test, treatment of a friend, exercising, doing your best, doing everything within your power to achieve your goals.

o Your thoughts: Your judgements about others and your judgements of yourself.

o Your perceptions: How you perceive something versus the facts.

Not up to you / best left up to the universe / not worth trying to control:

o Other people's thoughts and judgements: That one girl who clearly doesn't like you despite never having had an actual conversation with you.

o Other people's actions: Someone having a bad day and being rude to you.

o Other people's perceptions: Someone not having the same opinions as you.

o The weather: Worrying today about the rain tomorrow.

o Death: Well, that one needs no example.

o Health: This one's tricky. It's beyond our control to

a certain extent, e.g. worrying today about getting cancer or another unpredictable illness tomorrow, but we can, of course, take measures to maintain our general health so that we feel well.

o Your genes: Learning to accept the skin you're in instead of wishing you were born with Adriana Lima's facial features.

o Wealth: Again, like health, this can swing both ways. We can't control winning the lottery or getting lucky or being made redundant, but we can control the development of personal and professional skills that give us the best possible chance of earning a decent income.

So. How much of what's in this 'not up to you' list have you been concerned with? For me, it was a lot. Realising that the weight on your shoulders is coming mostly from things that are beyond your control and serving only to fuel your anxiety is eye-opening. Realising that you can choose to let go of it all is life-changing.

 **Exercise 1**
CONTROL EXERCISE
....

Write down your top concerns and worries right now. Tease apart what's worthy of your energy and attention by asking yourself: 'Is this something that is or is not within my control?' Sometimes, there will be aspects of one event that are within your control and aspects that are not, so write down both in a separate column. The former you can address. The latter? You need to let that sh't go. If you're finding that difficult, write the list of things that don't concern you on a separate piece of paper. Read it, scrunch it up and chuck it in the bin. There's a reason why ex-boyfriend burning parties are a thing (burning of their stuff, not the ex-boyfriend themselves); it's cathartic.

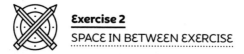

Exercise 2
SPACE IN BETWEEN EXERCISE

Recall past experiences where your emotions caused you to react without space in between. Write down what you did, how you behaved, how it affected you. In the middle, revisit that time and write down what the space in between might have allowed for. Using a table like the one below in your notebook, write down what would have been a better action or behaviour for you.

Feelings/Thoughts/Initial emotions	
Space in between/Logic and reason /Remove emotion	
Actions/Behaviour	

2. Take action

Thinking before you act is one thing. Remembering to act when action is required is something else completely. This element of stoicism is really important.

Though we might think of stoic philosophy and conjure up images in our mind's eye of dusty old books and long Gandalf-like beards and days spent sitting there theorising about life while looking out a rain-dappled window, the best stoics were actually doers. They got sh*t done. Explained by *The Daily Stoic*, this is what separates stoicism from other existing schools of thought: it has a practical purpose that we can apply to our lives – it's not a 'purely intellectual enterprise'.[46]

The thing is, you can read all the motivational books you want and have all of this knowledge and insight and theory swirling around in your brain, but until you go out into the world and apply it to your life, it's good for nothing. Stoicism is not about saying, 'Okay, well, since nothing is up to me, I may as well sit back and chill.' It's about prioritising your own actions and behaviours which, we now know, are well within your control. That's why I'm a big fan of introducing an idea or a concept and then offering a practical experiment so that you can put it to use and see if it works for you. This is why CBT (Cognitive Behavioural Therapy), which is experiment-based and incredibly practical, works so well for so many people and why I've found it so invaluable.

CBT is a talking therapy that helps to change the way you think and behave. It centres on the belief that our thoughts, feelings and behaviours are interrelated. In fact, it might be argued that CBT is the modern-day stoicism (sometimes referred to as 'scientific stoicism').

Try as you might, confidence is never going to increase until you put yourself into the situations that challenge it. Your comfort zone won't expand as a result of inertia. Your fear of failure won't be diminished until you confront what it is you fear. If nothing is changing for you, you have to ask yourself, what are you actually doing about it? Taking action, with this kind of information as a support along the way, is crucial. We can absolutely turn to these wise Greek men for tips on how to best live our lives or modern-day motivators like Tim Ferriss, but then we need to apply what we've learned.

Learn it, then live it.

> *'Knowledge, if it does not determine action, is dead to us.'*
> *Plotinus*

3. Mindfulness

Now, if all of this is sounding like practising stoicism requires ridding yourself of all emotion and acting like a robot, I've steered you wrong. Let's back up for a moment and introduce another fundamental principle of stoicism: mindfulness. Being stoic doesn't mean being cold or unfeeling or having no emotions whatsoever, it merely means not allowing yourself to be consistently guided by emotions. It's about rising above them when it comes to your behaviour. It's about domesticating your emotions. It's the original mindfulness.

I love that I'm a living, breathing, feeling, passionate and sometimes fiery person. I'm not particularly passive and I don't want to live life in monotone where I don't experience peaks and troughs. We can't expect ourselves to live like calm Greek philosophers (the original influencers) on a daily basis so don't go putting that kind of pressure on yourself. Sometimes, your emotions will rule the roost and that's okay. The thing about a stoic is that they will still feel strong emotions and always allow for them, but they will then decide to act based on reason. You can feel angry. You can curse at the wall and throw yourself on the floor like a toddler (in private), but you can then choose to act in what you know would be the best way to respond.

Sometimes, you will act out of anger or fear or worry; don't beat yourself up about it. Sometimes, I'll say no to something out of fear and then when I take a moment to let logic take the reins, I might regret my decision. This is where my impulsive nature can go a little against me and why my mother always tells me to sleep on things and to never write an emotion-fuelled email or a letter late at night. So, I try again next time. I reflect on my actions and I pick up where I left off. When you practise stoicism, for which mindfulness is a prerequisite, regularly, you'll learn to breathe into your feelings – stepping in to observe them and allow for them without being governed by them – before choosing to act out of logic and reason. If you can do this, then, I promise, you'll be happier with the outcome.

Exercise

CLASSIC MINDFULNESS EXERCISE

Next time you feel acutely nervous or anxious, sit with the feeling. Without panicking, bring your awareness into yourself – how you feel, what you're thinking – even if it's uncomfortable. Breathe in for four and out for eight, five times in a row. This slows down your heart rate. Anchor yourself by bringing your attention right down to your feet and the lower half of your body. Feel the ground underneath you as you breathe in and out, feel the chair if you are sitting.

Exercise

STOICISM CONFIDENCE RITUAL

Something these Ancient Greek dudes did was to sit down every evening and reflect on the day they had just lived. This is what they called 'balancing life's books each day'. So you might have felt like you had a sh'tty day or been a loser or failed in some way, but you go through the positives and negatives, what you learned and what you did well, what you might do better. This is the accumulation of evidence that will support your confidence when unhelpful and distorted thoughts begin to creep in.

4. Perspective

Another great stoic exercise is to remind yourself of how small you are (not in a literal sense) and how short life is. This is something we rarely feel (because we want to feel important) but, when you do it, it makes you more proactive in the moment that you're in.

Marcus Aurelius was a big fan of this and he was the Emperor of Rome so you can imagine it would be quite easy for him to get a big head and get carried away with his ego. This is not an exercise to make you feel less worthy – God, no – but to gain perspective on how fleeting life is, to feel humble and refocus your attention on what's important, away from the trivia that isn't.

When it comes to the fear of failure, we're so caught up in the moment and we apply far too much significance to an event that (a) won't matter in a few years' time and (b) won't add or take away from our happiness – provided we have our measures of self-worth and our core values sorted out. Even if we have great success or achievement, that itself is ephemeral. Gaining perspective from time to time will help you to find your balance, instilling you with confidence while diminishing your fear of failure. And should you ever find yourself on the flipside where you're getting a little too big for your boots, it will bring you back to your centre.

There's a great stoic story of Alexander the Great who everyone thought was the bee's knees having conquered the world - he even had several cities named after him, including Alexandria in Egypt. In terms of achievements, you couldn't get much bigger than that but one day, he got pissed and killed his best friend during a fight. He was never the same again and none of that previous achievement mattered to him. On paper, he had had a successful life, but from his personal standpoint, life was not successful. If you lose perspective (and, erm, kill someone as a result), who cares if there's a map with your name on it? None of that matters in the grand scheme of things.

It's not possible to have perspective all of the time because our lives and our experiences are relative to us - I, for one, have been known to burst into tears in a haze of hangriness - but when it all becomes too much, we can gently remind ourselves to spend some time considering the ephemeral nature of life. Everything is in flux. What we feel today, we might not feel tomorrow or in two weeks' time. The fear we feel today is not permanent.

I find it helps to ask myself this: 'Will this matter as much next week? Will I feel this way tomorrow?' When something feels enormous to you, remember that if our solar system were the size of a CD (old school, I know), the Milky Way galaxy would be the size of the Earth.

And the Milky Way is only one galaxy of billions that comprise the entire universe. In other words, we're tiny.

Our key stoic principles in summary:
- Focus on what you can control, let go of the rest
- Don't just learn, act
- Be mindful about your actions, be mindful of your emotions
- That thing you think of as incredibly significant - is it really?

Stoicism and confidence

Now that we've wrapped our heads around some of the most significant principles of stoicism, it should be pretty clear how this philosophy - when acted upon - can help in our quest to increase our self-confidence. For me, Massimo Pigliucci's words from *How To Be A Stoic* perfectly capture the direct impact that stoicism can have on our shared goal here: 'This is precisely the power of stoicism: the internalisation of the basic truth that we can control our behaviours but not their outcomes - let alone the outcomes of other people's behaviours - leads to the calm acceptance of whatever happens, secure in the knowledge that we have done our best given the circumstances.'[47]

If we're secure in the knowledge that we've done our best, we've come to terms with the unknown. If we're no longer plagued by uncertainty, we can feel confident about taking action, based on the things we can control. If you don't feel confident, it's either a case of not having done your best or prepared as best you can, *or* being overly concerned with things that are beyond your control. Pigliucci's words bring me back to the idea of comfortable neutrality, which we discussed on page 72.

Doing Your Best + Comfortable Neutrality = Confidence

Tool #2 –
The Importance Of
Goal-Setting

WE TEND TO talk about confidence and success in very general terms. We describe someone as a confident person or a not very confident person. Or we think of someone as successful or not. And while, yes, we want to feel confident in all areas of our lives, it's just too vague a goal. It's the same with the idea of being successful. For goals to be achievable, they have to be specific. Without having a clear picture of what it is we want, we have no focus and no sense of direction. Without setting particular goals, how can we tell if we are living the successful life we're aiming for?

Goals are measurable, goals give you a benchmark with which you can gauge how you're doing.

Someone might ask you if you feel that you are successful. You might have a million in the bank but not feel successful because money was never a goal of yours, but maybe doing that particular job that you wanted would have made you feel successful. So it all depends on what success means to you and the specific areas within your life. That's why, before you embark on any of the rest of the tools within this confidence toolkit, you must begin with goal-setting, a powerful tool in and of itself. Without something clear in your mind that you want to pursue or push through – for example, you might really want to push through your fear of public speaking – all of the other tools within this book will seem redundant.

You need to know why you're doing this, what you want to get out of it, and where you want to be in as specific a way as you can manage. You need something onto which the tools can be applied.

So knowing that goal-setting is important is one thing. Setting the goal is another and taking the steps necessary to achieve it is another thing again. It's not as simple as saying, 'I want to be a millionaire' (though we've all said this to ourselves and hoped that thinking it would just become our reality). Smart goal-setting is an exercise that you should spend a considerable amount of time on (and a pen and paper are essential).

First and foremost, you need to reflect on where you are right now. Which areas of your life are you confident about? Which areas are you not? Assess your current levels of satisfaction. In order to determine where you want or need to go, you need to know where you are. This initial evaluation will make the rest a lot easier.

Secondly, you have to revisit your idea of success. What does it look like to you? Then, you need to assess whether or not your ideas of success are something that truly motivate you. Again, you might think success equals money, but does having a lot of money, even if it means working seventy-hour weeks, actually motivate you? Or will you give up and move on to something else halfway through? Think of your goal in terms of what is important to you – ignoring everyone else – and why this particular goal would be valuable to you.

Don't just write down the goal, write down the why too. If you strive towards more money when it doesn't really interest you, you won't have the get up and go to make it happen. So get rid of any conditioned ideas of what success means in society, focus on what it means to you.

Then, don't merely think in terms of 'I'd like this or that'. You'll end up with far too long a list of goals, most of which you'll never get around to (think of how many New Year's resolutions you set yourself only to forget what they were and move on to the next ten things you'd like to do). You should have a strong feeling of having or needing to do something, and in determining your goals you need to consider what in your life would be a high priority. Try and limit yourself to key goals (perhaps three personal goals, three professional goals). Clarify them as much as you can by asking yourself: 'How will I go about achieving this?', 'What do I want to get from this?'

Mindtools.org[48] offers some great advice on how to set smart goals, but, essentially, the idea is to be specific and realistic. Are your goals actually attainable? The website also recommends going so far as to add a timescale to your goals. This might be hard, but give them a deadline. Think of yourself as a business – it only get to where it needs to be with a detailed business plan. What do you want and where do you want to be in six months, twelve months, eighteen months? Going into this detail will act as a great motivator – but, again, be realistic, otherwise you'll feel unnecessarily pressured. If you set outrageously unrealistic goals, you will only feel like sh*t when you struggle to reach them. Sure, you should set goals that aren't too easy and require work and effort, but with work and effort they should be within your reach.

For example, a realistic goal for me in the coming years might be to embark on a psychology course (what with all this book-writing and research). An unrealistic goal would be to run a marathon in less than three hours when I have no interest in running. A realistic goal for me a few years ago, when I was really grappling with anxiety, was to go out for dinner without having a panic attack. An unrealistic goal back then was to go backpacking alone around the world. Everyone's goals will differ.

When setting your goals keep your ideal lifestyle in mind. I try to keep my goal-setting in line with the kind of life I want to lead. I definitely do not want to live to work – I am just not that kind of person – so my goals will always be informed by that. I also try to keep my goals relevant by focusing on my strengths and what I'm good at. Aligning your goals with your strengths will be further motivation because you will have a sense of 'I can totally do this'.

Another insightful tool that goes against the traditional goal-setting grain is this: instead of only thinking about what you want, think about what you are willing to sacrifice. Don't just consider the end result but whether or not you are willing to accept the sacrifices involved to achieve your goal. This can be an uncomfortable task, but it helps you to confront the reality of what it is you want. For example, I am unwilling to put myself through a gruelling corporate seventy-hour week in order to have X amount in my bank account, therefore it's not a goal for me. Yes, we all think having a gold medal would be nice, but are you prepared to live the life of an Olympian in training? Nah. All rewards come with costs, so it's good to be aware of what those might be before you embark on something that you won't be into halfway through.

Mindtools.org also recommends using 'I will' statements when setting your goals, rather than 'I would like to'. This helps you to visualise actually doing it and getting there. The former kind of statement has more power and instils more confidence, whereas the latter sounds like something that you don't believe you can get to.

When you're clear on your goal, set yourself a detailed action plan.

Let's take one of my personal goals as an example. This is how I set about trying to become comfortable with public speaking and delivering corporate presentations.

Decide how the goal is to be measured. →	The goal will be measured by me and how well I think I've done, and partly by feedback from the organisers.

What, if any, are the practical steps necessary to achieve your goal?

→ I will take classes with a voice coach to learn how to control my breathing and modulate my voice. I will put myself out there with corporate companies and let them know I'm available, which will be scary at first!

Can you break the overall goal down into smaller goals? This will make it feel even more doable.

→ Yes. I will first put myself in a panel experience, where I am on a stage with others and not entirely alone. This will be a stretch-zone experience. I will then give a talk to a small group by myself, working my way up to a much bigger talk (where I am definitely in the learning zone but, hopefully, experiencing optimal anxiety).

What will it take to get to the end line?	→ Lots of practice in front of the mirror (comfort zone), then several smaller experiences public speaking, lots of time spent preparing for each talk. Lots of comfortable neutrality, learning to be okay with the unknown.

Then, set reminders to check back in with the goals you've set from time to time. How are you doing? Have you knocked anything off your list and therefore you should celebrate your success?	→ Yes, I have learned a lot about the right way to breathe when giving a presentation. I am feeling more proactive having taken the initial steps and I have scheduled a talk for the coming month, and I'm using this toolkit to see it through.

Does this goal still remain high on your list?	→ Yes, public speaking has always been a big one for me.

It's worth being mindful when new goals come into your life. This can sometimes mean that you will now have less focus on an existing goal. Are you being pulled in another direction? Goal competition – when goals compete for your time and energy – is a big thing, and can be majorly off-putting, so be ruthless with what you are pursuing. Typically, you'll do best if you can focus on one thing at a time. Life may take you in unexpected directions, which means your goals and what you value may change, so remember that this is something you can adapt as you go. Like everything else in this book, it's part of a work in progress.

One of the most motivating and confidence-boosting things we can experience is evidence of our progress. So, remember, even if you don't achieve the end result, mark down the things you learned or changed about your life while trying to get there; achieving any level of personal development should be viewed as a success.

Taking this proactive step to map out your goals and the action plan that will get you there (which can be broken down in terms of smaller, more bitesize goals) puts you in control of your situation, laying the foundations for resilience and self-confidence. Goal-setting is empowering. Setting goals with confidence gives you an initial boost to follow through.

Goal guide

- Without goals we have no focus – we cannot expect to just become more successful or more confident without them.
- Write down your goals somewhere that you can revisit them easily.
- Narrow them down to specifics.
- Be sure not to set too many and wide-ranging goals.
- Ask yourself why you want to achieve these goals.
- Consider what you'll have to sacrifice in achieving your goals.
- Use 'I will' wording, framing your goals positively.
- Be time-specific too – give your goals a timeframe.
- Don't skip the action plan.
- Revisit it often.
- Celebrate progress.

Tool #3
Taking Fear As A
Signal To Act

BECAUSE OF THE WAY our brains work, our natural reaction is to run when we feel fear. Or it might be to say 'no' without giving it any thought and opt out of something if it's our emotional safety that feels threatened. You might refer to fear as an acronym for 'F*ck Everything And Run'. This is fine when there is a genuine threat (physical or emotional) but what do we do when there isn't? A good many of us won't question whether a fear is real or perceived. We don't give it a second thought and we do whatever it takes to get away from the negative feelings because, naturally enough, they're not nice to feel. But this knee-jerk reaction to fear is one of the reasons why we find it so hard to increase our confidence and why we feel that fear always gets the better of us and keeps us stuck. If you've picked up this book, it's because you want to break out of this misinformed state.

What we need to do is flip the paradigm. Is fear really all that bad?

Question it. Consider it. Maybe the terrifying thing from which we are running is not a vicious, rabid dog, but a puppy in need of reassurance. Since learning that fear was going to be there whether I like it or not – and being the generally anxious person that I am – I decided to take the feelings of fear as a loud call to action. I now take it as a roadmap. The kind of fear we feel when we're really afraid to fail because we care points us in the direction of that which is important to us. Acting like rocket fuel, it brings our focus right into parts of our lives that perhaps need improving, it helps us to hone in on things that matter to us – it even directs us towards our goals. This is why people say: 'If you're not scared, you're doing it wrong.'

I used to try my best to squash down my fear whenever it popped up (like closing the lid on a jack-in-the-box); making excuses on behalf of my fear was a full-time job. If something presented itself that sent a jolt of panic through my mind and body – at one point it would have been the mere suggestion of a trip abroad – I would scramble to think of a reason to opt out, other than to just say, 'I'm scared.'

These were excuses I'd not only use with others but I would also try to convince myself that, for example, 'I better not go to this thing because I was planning on giving my dog a bath.' I wasn't afraid of flying, but I was afraid of being away from home – out of my literal comfort zone. In fact, I would sooner hope a volcano erupted, rendering all airports redundant, than have to face my fear and say, 'Okay, what is this actually about?' or 'Is this something you want to work through?'

If, like me, you don't want fear to hold you back, then you will accept that most of the time, this has been the case. Now, when I feel that part of me want to run for the onesie and dive under the covers, this is what I do:

1 I stop. Instead of being paralysed by it, I decide to process it. Is this fear really a bad thing? Does it deserve all of the negative connotations?

2 I acknowledge the feelings and accept them. Fear is normal and natural and unavoidable. I try to get a better sense of where it's coming from and why I'm feeling it. Fear often comes as a result of not under-standing. What exactly am I afraid of?

3 I ask myself, 'Are you feeling scared because this is something that you actually want to do?'

4 Is your fear response an indication that it's time to act?

5 Is there actually a threat to your safety, emotional or physical?

6 Could the fear be excitement? My body has a hard time telling the difference.

7 Is the fear not the worst feeling ever but actually a form of inner fuel?

8 Is this a challenge that you want to rise to?

9 I remind myself that there are two selves within me: the childlike self who will see fear as a negative, and the adult self who will see opportunity. Which self will I go with?

10 Is the fear pointing me towards an area of my life in which fear has been holding me back?

11 Do I want to take the next steps to address this fear so that it no longer holds me back?

12 I also remind myself of the nature of fear: that it overrides intelligence and negates the facts. Fear is emotion.

13 I remind myself that fear is useful. It's going to ensure that I'm prepared, it's not going to hinder me if I decide to move forward, and it will probably make me perform better (no matter what I'm doing).

14 If I took fear out of the equation, would I want to do it?

15 Having processed my fears, they'll probably still be there – don't expect to feel fearless – but, instead of trying to get over them, I get *into* them. There is one more question to ask yourself: 'Can I use this to my advantage?'

Instead of seeing fear itself as the threat and the reason to avoid things, decide that, from now on, fear itself is a tool within your confidence kit.

So, **F***ck **E**verything **A**nd **R**un?

Or

Face It, **E**xplore It, **A**ccept It And **R**ise Above It?

Tool #4 – Taking Your Fears For A Run

ALLOWING FOR WORRIES, concerns, fear and moments of panic is an important part of your strategy for building confidence. I've always found that burying feelings of worry and pretending they're not there is a recipe for disaster. Remember, our goal is not to try and feel fearless or to get to a point where the fears aren't there at all, but to manage our fears so that they're no longer a roadblock in the way of success.

After acknowledging the existence of your fears or that which has taken your self-confidence hostage, you must then exercise your fears (i.e. sending your fears out for a run until such time as they've run out of steam and are thus less powerful). This is something I've always done (essentially allowing myself to have a meltdown until there's no melting left to do), and I recently came across a similar approach to this in a brilliant book called *The Chimp Paradox* by Dr Steve Peters.[49] In his critically acclaimed and somewhat quirky text, Peters offers a mind-management model for which you must accept his idea that within every person there is a rational adult, which he calls 'the human', and a worrisome, not always rational self, which he calls 'the chimp'. The chimp is his simple way of characterising the limbic part of our brains (in which you'll find the amygdala and our innate survival instincts) while the human covers the frontal lobe where we have logic and reason. Any and all of our difficulties, explains Peters, arise when the chimp and the human clash. The chimp reacts first, going on how it feels right here, right now to decide on future actions whereas the human makes decisions based on what needs to be done - what the right thing to do is when you take emotion out of the equation - and how he or she will feel at the end of the day when they look back on how they used their time. Two very different approaches, but there has to be room for both.

His book details the various ways in which we must understand the nature of the chimp and manage it so that it doesn't manage us. Sometimes, the chimp is right on the money - if it starts to freak out as you're about to jump off a cliff, for example - but a lot of the time, this emotional machine is sending false alarms because it would much rather remain peaceful and comfortable.

This part of your brain is neither good nor bad, it just is. You shouldn't try to switch it off entirely – after all, it has a lot of uses – but you must know when to take it at its word and when to override it. Peters says that whenever you have feelings, thoughts or behaviours that you do not want, you've been hijacked by your chimp. One of Peters' suggestions is that when your chimp is worried or having an absolute conniption, you mustn't try to quieten it without giving it the room to express its concerns. This would be similar to rolling your eyes at a child who is fearful about something that you're fine with. To them, it's scary, so it wouldn't be right to belittle it. Instead, you nurture it. You allow for this and, eventually, the chimp (like a child) runs out of steam. What's left is the logical adult who says, 'Okay, are you done?' and can either accept or reject the chimp's suggestions (such as saying no to an opportunity that takes you outside of your comfort zone).

When you are about to take a step outside of your comfort zone, your chimp (your limbic brain) will be agitated. It gets emotional, it feels fear, it goes into protection mode. The first thing you have to do here is release the emotion. The reason you do this is to reassure the part of you that is scared – it needs to know that you're listening and that you take it seriously, otherwise it will start to make even more of a racket. Think about it: when you are really upset and you talk things over with someone, it helps to calm you down. In the same way, exercising your fears with yourself - even if you have to take out a pen and paper or unload it onto someone else who is willing - calms you right down.

When you've let all of this stream out - however long it takes - you are in a better position to listen to logic and reason, which will then help you to make the best decision about what to do next.

So whatever you do, when you feel fearful about something, don't rush to force positive and rational thoughts on yourself. Allow yourself to freak the f*ck out even if it feels counterintuitive. When I was experiencing crippling anxiety, I worried that dwelling on it more by discussing it would only make it worse, but research shows there is a lot to be gained from expressing yourself (even if it's just in front of the mirror).

Research shows that simply talking through and labelling our fears (especially phobias) can help to lessen the negative arousal. One UCLA study focused on people with a fear of spiders.[50] The researchers asked them all to approach a Chilean rose-haired tarantula and touch it. They then divided the sample into four groups. The first was the effect-labelling group, who were instructed to verbalise how they felt emotionally about the exercise (e.g. 'I am incredibly anxious that this disgusting tarantula will crawl all over me'). The second, the reappraisal group, were asked to talk about the experience in non-emotional terms and simply state the facts (e.g. 'the spider is behind a glass box'). The third group were a distraction group and were asked to say something unrelated to the spider (e.g. 'it's raining today'). The fourth group were the control group and were given no instructions.

Interestingly, the first group showed a physiological change. They showed less negative arousal (which they tested via skin conductance) than the other groups. They were also more willing to interact with the spider than the other groups, having expressed themselves emotionally. The more fear and anxiety words they used to describe their fear, the more they seemed to get over their fear of spiders. Other studies referenced in *Psychology Today* have shown that when students were asked to write down their worries ten minutes before taking a high-stakes test, their test performance increased. The students with the most anxiety about the test went from a B- to a B+.

Research aside, I've found this really works for me. Think of sitting down with a loved one and them saying to you, 'Okay, tell me all about it.' They have to listen and engage without passing any judgement on your concerns until you've finished. Then, they will offer rational advice: either agreeing that what you are worried about is absolutely warranted and you should step away, or gently helping you to realise that most of your worries are, in fact, irrational.

In short, get things off your chest. Don't swallow your fears and worries. Verbalising your fear helps to ensure it won't pop up later at an inopportune time.

Exercise
EXERCISE YOUR FEARS

Think of something that requires you to go outside of your comfort zone, something that you know would be good to do but instantly makes you feel worried and fearful. Take out a pen and paper and write down every single concern you have, no matter how ridiculous it sounds. Write it all down until you have nothing left to write. Think of everything that might come up, any fears you might have on the day that you might not think about until then.

Then, go back over everything with a highlighter. Pretend you are someone else reading it, deciding what is rational and what is not. Take the rational points and figure out what can be done to help with these concerns. For example, if one of your worries is that you will forget what you're going to say, one of your solutions would be preparation, which is one of our upcoming steps.

Tool #5 – The 'F*ck It' Moment and the Art of Decision-Making

IT'S TIME NOW to introduce one of my favourite tools. It's a particular profane delight and something with which anyone who's ever pushed themselves outside of their comfort zone will be familiar: the 'f*ck it' moment.

The 'f*ck it' moment is the ultimate expression of assertiveness in the face of fear. You know that feeling when you have worked through your never-ending list of reasons *not* to do something that you know, deep down, you *should* do? This is where I like to think of myself as having two selves – the childlike self that feels fear strongly and says 'Nope! No f*cking way, don't even ask me, the answer is no', and the higher, more adult self that just quietly knows better, even if it doesn't always speak up. On a good day, despite your abundance of fear and worry and, perhaps, empirical evidence to the contrary, your higher self steps in and overrides the childlike self – without completely negating its worries – and says, quite simply, 'F*ck it, I am going to do this', 'I am going to get through this'. This, I assure you, is a very powerful moment.

In my own experience, one of the most crucial steps in confronting fear and allowing for an expansion of my comfort zone is the simple act of making a decision (and when you make that decision, you simply say 'f*ck it', out loud, provided you're not in the company of the easily offended). Yes, you still feel nervous, you still take your concerns seriously – these are all real and justifiable feelings, don't get me wrong – but when you make a decision to do something and tell yourself and those around you that you are going to do it, you instil in yourself a surge of confidence that enables you to approach the cliff's edge, so to speak. It really works. When this happens, you realise pretty quickly that a lot of your fear and anxiety is wrapped up in indecision and hesitation – and this is common to us all. The confidence comes from your ability to just trust yourself and take the leap of faith. If you can feel all of those worries and, at the end of the day, say 'f*ck it', you can absolutely survive, and perhaps even thrive. It might not be the desired amount of confidence necessary to sail through, but it's enough to help you show up at the starting line.

The Four No's from Richard Templar's
The Rules of Life.

1 **No fear**
2 **No surprise**
3 **No hesitation**
4 **No doubt**

I first came across a version of this concept in Richard Templar's *The Rules of Life.*[51] These days, it's a permanent fixture on my bedside table (it's one of those books you can dip in and out of when you need a little pep talk).

For one particular rule, he cites a seventeenth-century samurai warrior who had a four-point philosophy for a successful life. The first was 'no fear', which was to decide that his life would be a lot easier if he let go of his fears. Well, that one's easier said than done, pal. The second was 'no surprise', and this has always stuck with me. If you are awake and aware, not a whole lot in life can creep up on you out of the blue. Mindfulness helps a lot in this regard as it teaches us how to be aware of ourselves and our surroundings on a daily basis. Had I been truly awake and aware of what was happening in my life when I first became acutely ill as a result of anxiety, it might not have got so bad in the first place – scratch that, it *definitely* wouldn't have got so bad. What's more, I repeatedly said to myself, 'I just don't *know* what happened, this came out of *nowhere*, I was fine and then I was suddenly very not fine.' Listen, this is exactly what can happen if we spend too long in the success zone and then, unbeknownst to ourselves, wind up in the panic zone. I don't like to admit it, but the anxiety was coming for me based on my lifestyle choices at that time, and there were plenty of warning signs that I *chose* not to pay attention to. In this sense, there are fewer surprises in life than we first thought or, at least, there are fewer surprises than we are willing to admit to. If you are aware, not a whole lot can creep up on you. If you are truly awake in a relationship, it won't surprise you or shock you when it ends, there will have been signs along the way that something had gone awry.

Nobody wants to confront the truth on a daily basis. This is really important when it comes to personal development too but, obviously, there are things in life we cannot control that will absolutely occur out of the blue. With the elements that you *can't* control, we practise stoicism (jump back to Chapter 8 for a refresher). With the elements that you *can* control, however, be sure to be awake – really awake, with no blinkers on – and you'll rarely be caught unawares. Also, know that whatever your situation now, it's going to change. If it's good, it will change (not necessarily for the worse). If it's bad, it will change too. This ebb and flow of life shouldn't come as a surprise. And we should be glad that it happens. Yes, we'd have a lot less unpredictability about which to be fearful, but we would also be bored as f*ck.

The third and fourth points of his code for a successful and contented life are the most relevant to what we're discussing here and I've never forgotten them: 3. 'no hesitation' and 4. 'no doubt'. Consider them your calls to action.

The former is like the 'f*ck it' moment, though I suspect a seventeenth-century samurai warrior rarely used the f-word as easily as I do now. Essentially, you still allow yourself the time to run through all of your fears and worries and things that could go wrong and reasons not to do something, and then you make a decision. Only you – your higher-thinking self – can know if it's worth doing or whether it's actually a bad idea that won't serve you well. Sometimes it *is* a bad idea, and we'll get to that later. But spend too long thinking about it and the opportunity might pass you by.

The fourth point – no doubt – is equally important. This is about not questioning your decision when you've made it. When you have committed yourself to a certain path – either opting in or opting out – don't go over it again and again in your head. And don't look back. Don't second guess yourself, don't try to justify anything. You don't have to be necessarily confident in what you're about to do, that will come with experience and repetition and lots of incremental comfort-zone stretching, but you should be confident in your decision. You've made one, and that, in itself, is hard enough. Sometimes, that's the hardest part. Practising this kind of self-assertion, even if at first you don't quite believe yourself, is crucial on the path to building confidence.

For me, when I am circling around the idea of doing something, I am riddled with unhelpful thoughts telling me to run a million miles away and choose a career with less room for the unpredictable. The negatives always come first, along with a surge of unwanted physical feelings, usually in my stomach (which then, unfortunately, finds itself in my throat). I will always feel this way at first, no matter what I take on or how much cliff-jumping I do, because my body's automatic response is always to protect itself from anything that disturbs my status quo or threatens my physical or emotional security. And that's okay, we shouldn't try to change that, it's what makes us human. But when I make a decision to go forward with something, it actually dissipates a significant amount of the fear, especially those nasty physical feelings.

The thing is, I'm not just faking it till I make it, by doing this, I've actually set about creating the biology of confidence. For me, indecision breeds fear, whereas going for it quells it, to a certain extent.

What's really interesting to observe when you find yourself in this situation is to see where you stand with 'the fear of the fear'. Here's what I mean: If you make a decision and you feel that the anxiety has lifted somewhat, you'll know that a lot of what you were fearing was the fear itself. The task at hand, whatever shape that may take for you, is now not as unnerving.

While at this point, a large part of me still admittedly wants to find a way out and hide under a duvet or conveniently fall ill or, you know, get hit by a truck, the benefits of the 'f*ck it' moment should, and usually do, come out on top. For me, they are as follows:

1 I've made a decision, so I no longer have to torture myself with 'will I, won't I' questioning.

2 I will feel a thrill and a surge of excitement in knowing that because I have chosen to do this in spite of my fears, I will become a better version of myself. Pushing yourself through fear like this actually releases a stream of dopamine into the body. A nice side-effect you had overlooked.

3 When I say I am going to do something, and I vocalise this and commit, I convince my childlike self that it will be okay. It needs reassurance and it listens.

4 I feel proud of myself for being brave, which gives me a further surge of confidence to follow through. I feel proud for just showing up. I think of how I'm going to get through the situation which has created

so many feelings of fear and this makes me feel in control. Like a boss. And there's nothing like feeling you're the one in control to give you confidence.

5 Making a decision puts me in control. Fear is most often linked with the feeling of not having control but this gives it right back to you.

6 In making a decision, I've already instilled confidence, even before I've taken on the task itself. This, alone, is an expansion of my comfort zone and that in itself is already a success.

Don't dawdle

So, the act of asserting yourself and making decisions is a very important building block on the road to confidence, but it's also important that we do this quickly. Yes, it's still important to walk through the fears, concerns, thoughts, worst-case scenarios, best-case scenarios, and potential and believable excuses for opting out, so that they don't come back to haunt you at an inopportune time later on, but you should put a time limit on this assessment part. You don't want to ignore your childlike self but you also can't indulge it too much, otherwise its tantrum will only snowball into panic and then it will be very hard to think straight and know what is reasonable and what is blown out of proportion because of stress. Making a decision *without too much delay* will prevent this from happening – it works for me, and it will get you to that point of confidence a lot sooner, saving you lots of unnecessary anguish.

What I'm hoping you realise by now is that decision is the very powerful bridge between your thoughts and your actions. However, I appreciate that you may be like me, and therefore quite anxiety-prone, so it may take a little practice to get comfortable with the art of decision-making. It is a skill, but one that can absolutely be learned. What's more, fear and anxiety will tend to bend you in favour of a decision that gives you the safest outcome. In this case, to ensure your anxiety isn't always the one in the driving seat of decision-making, I find it very useful to write a dual list of reasons to do something and reasons not to do something. This means I'm looking at it from a balanced and reasonable perspective. I'm not trying to be something I'm not – fearless – but I'm giving myself the fair assessment I deserve. I complete the exercise at the end of the chapter.

Say, for example, I go back to a time when I was asked to go on a TV current affairs panel show that's live, very serious and discussion-based. The guests who appear on this show are extremely well educated, well informed and highly qualified in their areas of expertise (I, on the other hand, felt like I was none of these things – hello, imposter syndrome). On this particular day, that was my mountain to climb, but the process of facing the fear will be the same whether you're about to ask somebody out on a date or say yes to a new job. It's crucial that you know that all of these tools are transferable.

The panel discussion was on mental health reform in government policy and education, and even though I've written a bestselling book on how to manage anxiety, the nature of the show was still very much beyond my comfort zone. I was only getting used to being interviewed and now I was entering what I perceived to be the lion's den.

This is what happened to me.

I was asked about it in person, face to face, and they wanted me to appear on the show that same night. No time to prepare! No time to freak out! No time to obsess and mull over and indulge my fears and then arrive at a reasonable decision in my own time. This was both good and bad. *Good* because I wouldn't have to spend a whole week worrying, and *bad* because I'm a big believer in preparation (more on that later). I felt pressured into saying yes on the spot to avoid an awkward conversation but, then, on my drive home, I instantly felt consumed with fear and self-doubt. I wasn't alone in the car, every negative feeling I could muster carpooled with me all the way home. Anxiety rode shotgun, with a speech bubble suspended in the air that said, 'You're going to fail.' The minute I got home, I contacted my nearest and dearest, voicing my concerns. They told me it was up to me. They told me not to feel pressured into it but that if I did do it, I'd be fine.

I didn't believe them.

I then phoned the person who had asked me to go on the show and told her that there was just no way I could do this – 'I'm not good enough' was the gist of the reason I gave her for opting out. I felt a little bit safer, but there was also the feeling of having let myself down bubbling underneath. Luckily, she pushed back, in a gentle way, telling me that I absolutely could do this and not only would I be well capable, I would be a wonderful addition for them – 'A breath of fresh air,' she said. Then, the words 'Okay, I'll do it' just came out of my mouth. I probably said 'f*ck it' too because she sounded like the kind of producer who wouldn't mind that.

All of my concerns were still there, but I knew I had decided to commit and at precisely that moment, all of the fears stopped fighting for airspace and said, 'Oh, okay, she's doing it, we're obviously not getting our way here.' The debate was over and the anxiety sort of settled.

I then got texts and calls from those to whom I had been talking: 'Well? Did you decide to opt out?' Like a different person, I said, 'No, I'm gonna do it. I'll be fine.' And I wasn't just *saying* this, I really felt it. I arrived at the studio later that night (way past my normal bedtime) and while I still had jitters, I did not want to run for the door; that's because I had made a decision. Long story short, I got through it. I even spoke up to voice my opinion that went against everyone else's on the panel, which I thought was brave. An extra dose of 'you've got this' stirred. I felt like a duck with my feet flapping vigorously underneath the water, but to those watching me at home who knew of my turmoil that day, it appeared as though I had always had my sh*t together.

Fear often dominates decisions - it's always the first to arrive at the party - but making a decision tells fear where to shove it.

Exercise
COST/BENEFITS ANALYSIS

*This exercise is nothing new if you're as voracious a self-help book reader as I am, but it's as relevant today as ever. Think of the next potential opportunity on the horizon that makes you feel uneasy. Draw a line down the middle of a piece of paper. To the left of the line write down the list of reasons **not** to do it and then, on the right, the reasons **to** do it.*

Here's where I add in my own twist: even if you don't yet feel like opting in, try to write more reasons to do it than not to do it, so that the pros list appears longer than the cons list. Don't just make stuff up, but make a conscious effort to focus on the possible positive outcomes.

Always do the negatives first so the reasons not to do it are off your chest and not bursting to get out. Let them have their moment and then move on to the reasons for something.

The result is a good visual motivator for me – it's measured, it considers both sides and it shows you that there are more benefits (short term and long term) than disadvantages to be gleaned from the situation. You might not feel ready yet, but you can't argue with numbers. It makes things feel like less of a risk because, clearly, you've got more to gain than you have to lose. When you've done that, proceed to ticking the box you feel best fits with your own results.

Reasons not to do it

....

1 I'm not prepared or in control of the situation.

2 I'm not sure what they will discuss.

3 I don't feel competent among these people.

4 I am the youngest and least experienced.

5 I am not qualified.

6 I might say something stupid.

7 If I say something wrong, I will tarnish my reputation.

8 I feel far too nervous to do this.

9 I won't be able to articulate myself.

10 I might have a panic attack.

11 I'm afraid if it doesn't go well I will never feel brave enough to do this again.

Reasons to do it

....

1 They have asked for me specifically.

2 They must think I'm more than capable.

3 I'm a bestselling author on the subject of mental health, why shouldn't I feel worthy of being there?

4 I have been on TV before and it's been fine.

5 I am actually more capable than I feel on the inside.

6 This is a good opportunity for my career.

7 This is a good opportunity to stretch my comfort zone.

8 If it goes okay I will feel so much more confident in myself.

9 If it goes okay I will have expanded my comfort zone for the better.

10 I am in control of the situation to a certain extent – I can choose my words.

11 I will be so glad I did it.

12 I will make my loved ones proud.

13 I will make myself proud.

14 It will be yet another case of Caroline 1, Fear 0

☐

☐

No, maybe next time.

*F*ck it, let's do it.*

Tool #6 – The Secret To Temptation Bundling

TEMPTATION BUNDLING is a very useful tool within your fear-facing/confidence-building arsenal. It's a strategy I use *all* the time when my stomach starts to gurgle and my amygdala says, 'No way am I doing that.'

I first came across it when listening to a Freakonomics podcast[52] in which the idea of temptation bundling was introduced as the ultimate solution when willpower alone isn't enough. It involves linking something you'd rather not do, which requires willpower and which we'll call A, with something that would make it all worthwhile in the end, which we'll call B. You want to get to B, so you go through A.

Coined by Katherine Milkman, researcher at the University of Pennsylvania, she explains it as the act of combining a highly enjoyable, low-beneficial activity with a less enjoyable but highly beneficial activity.[53] An example might be cleaning the kitchen now, so I can then sit down and binge on *The Crown* later. It helps to push you over the edge when you'd look for any reason not to do something. It also makes the treat so much more enjoyable, because you feel you've earned it.

For me, it's particularly helpful when applied to anything that asks me to go outside my comfort zone, where an element of fear (or in some cases, a great deal of fear) is at play. When I'm about to do something and I'm riddled with fear, I build in a treat at the other end and it makes a huge difference: the temptation waves at me from the other side of fear and I walk, head held high, to reach it.

For Milkman, it's all about attaching a 'want' to a 'should'. 'I *should* give this speech because I will learn from it and more than likely my confidence will increase. I *want* a Big Mac meal, so I'll do that afterwards.' The shoulds are things we tend to avoid – and fear is often the biggest inhibitor – but the wants make it that bit easier, by working as motivation. When you do this often enough, it makes you more likely to engage in the 'should' behaviour, and it's that very action of facing it that will serve to bolster your self-confidence.

When writing my list of topics to include in this book, I kept referring to this part as 'chicken', inspired by my dog, Bear. (He's a cross between a Shih Tzu and Pomeranian; some people refer to the mix as a Shiranian, but I prefer to call him my little Pom Sh*t and I like to imagine that he's Instagram's rising star.) At about eight or nine months of age, Bear seemed to develop a lot of anxiety (and they say owners and their dogs become more alike every day). For no apparent reason, he suddenly feared going for a walk, despite the fact that he had loved it up until that point. When I was done worrying about having transferred all of my own fear and angst onto him, I wondered what might help him face his fears, so that we could get back to our daily walking routine and so that I could get back some semblance of sanity and not have to exercise the dog within the four walls of my house. What does Bear want? What would he do just about anything for? Chicken. Even if he was bathing in a sea of smelly socks (for which he has a devout passion) if he heard me say 'Chicken!', he'd be by my side before I'd finished saying the word. Chicken interrupts all of his behaviours and even his thought processes. Now, I know, we humans are a lot more complex, but it got me thinking about temptation bundling in action, albeit on a very simple level, which can work as a helpful aid in fear extinction (the opposite of fear conditioning, which we've discussed in Chapter 2).

I'd take Bear out for a walk and before we'd get to the end of the driveway, he'd crouch down, ears tucked behind his head, fear of God look in his eyes as he wondered why I would force him into such an apparently dangerous situation. Dragging him didn't help, that just increased his fear as he saw someone he trusted and loved forcing him to do something he wasn't comfortable with. But when I introduced temptation bundling – the literal dangling of a piece of chicken on the other side of the road, which he'd have to walk to to eat – more positive associations were made. He didn't think at all about the fear that had seemed to consume his little furry head. He wanted the damn chicken and he wanted it now. It was the ultimate motivation. Before long, he'd done the thing he was avoiding and he could reap both the short-term benefits of a tasty chicken treat and the longer-term benefits of having conquered his fear (if he has any concept of long-term benefits, that is). This was his temptation bundle.

Now I'm not sure any of us could love anything as much as Bear loves chicken, but when you're faced with a challenge that you want to run a million miles from, you have to set a temptation in place that can only be reached by going through it.

It makes sense that this would be a useful tool, but Milkman wanted to put it to the test, to prove its efficacy.

Her research was documented in the paper 'Holding the Hunger Games Hostage at the Gym', published in both the *NCBI* and *Management Science*.[54] For the study, Milkman split 226 students into three groups. Group one were given an iPod to listen to at the gym that came with pre-installed audio books that were generally believed to be page-turners (such as *The Hunger Games*). These guys listened to thirty minutes of the audio book while working out and they were not allowed to listen to any more than that unless they came back to the gym. The second group were similar but they had to rely on their own willpower. They had the books on their iPods, which they could bring home, but they were asked to listen to it only when exercising. The third group were the control and, apparently, were given a voucher for Barnes & Noble before they began working out and had the pleasure of listening to whatever they wanted at the gym. The results? The first group worked out 51% more frequently when they bundled their want with their should. The second group were 29% more likely to exercise than the control group but their workouts petered off over time.

Exercise

TEMPTATION BUNDLING EXERCISE

Make a list of shoulds (or, to be nicer to yourself, coulds), the things you might avoid but would benefit from. These are things that will probably not be enjoyable in the short term but which have more long-term benefits.

Then, write a list of corresponding wants (within reason) that could work as motivation. The wants should be things that give you instant gratification when you do them, without necessarily providing any long-term benefits, otherwise they won't work as motivation to do the first part. These are your bundles. Take one on right away – maybe it's as simple as folding away the clothes on your floor and then watching a YouTube video of puppies who are too fat and cuddly to stand up (works for me).

It definitely helps if the temptation isn't something you'd always do on a regular day, otherwise the impact of its motivation wanes. Essentially, your goal here is to incentivise yourself appropriately into doing things that will serve you well. If you're unsure about the shoulds column, just ask yourself, 'What would be good for my self-confidence that I don't really feel like doing?' Is there a fear you could face with an incentive? Is there something you keep procrastinating on?

Tool #7 – Sidestepping Your Way Around Fear

BEFORE MY FIRST BOOK came out, my anxiety (ironically) reached a high that I wasn't sure I could handle. Yes, I had got to a point of managing my anxiety on a day-to-day basis, but, no, I wasn't comfortable with the idea of going on TV and radio and talking about it with ease (I wanted to throw up in the interviewer's face, but my publicist advised against that). The thing is, just because I had written a book about anxiety didn't mean I was beyond it; I still had anxiety, this was not something that was in the past for me.

I was gearing up for some relatively high-profile interviews and was consumed by the utter fear that I would not be able to get the words out of my mouth. I did one phone interview with a small radio station and the nerves got the better of me. This was (at the time) confirmation that the bigger interviews would be a failure. I was so convinced of this but I needed to figure out a way through it. I instinctively thought to myself that I had to do something else, something that scared me but had a lot less consequence attached to it (when compared to the fears I had of making a total ass of myself on TV). I figured, if I could take my fear about one thing and temporarily redirect it onto another activity that I could do before I faced the really big stuff, maybe I'd experience a boost of confidence based on the fact that I'd thrown myself courageously into the deep end. I thought to myself, 'Well, you're already riddled with fear, you might as well knock something else off your list in the meantime.' If I survived this other task, I'd survive the one that was hanging over me, the one that, at that moment in time, mattered more than anything else. I now refer to this technique as 'sidestepping'.

What did I do? I went for a singing lesson. Joyful to others, terrifying to me. I was always talking about singing and wishing I had a voice like Mariah Carey even if just for singing in the shower. Turns out, my fiancé actually does listen when I'm jabbering on because he went and booked me a string of lessons for my birthday. It was something I had wanted to do but I didn't *want* to do it, when the chance to do it was right in front of me. It was something I'd get to 'someday', I'd always thought.

By saying I wanted to do it, it sounded like I was brave enough to try something that scared me, but I'd put it off for as long as I could.

I put it off for a year, blaming busyness and other things that would get in the way. I only considered giving it a shot in my hour of need, when I knew, somehow, that it would indirectly serve a purpose. Why was I so afraid? I was afraid to fail at it. Being a perfectionist, I wasn't okay with the idea of *developing* a skill from zero to ten – I just wanted to have it already. Stupid as it sounds, I was afraid of being judged by the singing teacher. I was afraid to be told, 'Sorry, love, but you have a sh*t voice and you should go back to the day job.' It's not that I ever wanted to sing professionally, but I wanted to be good at whatever I put my hand to. I was also afraid that going for singing lessons would mean I'd have to sing in front of other people, which I was never going to be okay with, unless I was polluted drunk, crowing in chorus with my friends at karaoke.

In a state of fear, I rang the singing teacher and told her of my impending doom. Turns out, she worked with lots of people on public speaking and a lot of what you learn in a singing lesson is, at least at the start, about breathing. Controlled breathing was as essential for interviews as it was for keeping my breakfast down. I booked a session with her for the following day. Here's what happened.

The minute I booked the lesson with her, my fear about everything else subsided somewhat. This was because I had taken action and proactively sought a way to address my fears. This alone was a confidence boost. I was no longer wallowing in it, I was facing it, even if it was in an indirect way. Then I went for the lesson. I unloaded my anxiety onto the poor woman and then we got down to work. I learned breathing techniques and mouth exercises to loosen up my voice and rid myself of tension. And then we started to sing. I could feel the fear rise in me again, but what was the consequence?

Could I live with the fact that maybe I wasn't Mariah Carey the second? Yes, I could. Was anything bad going to happen to me? No. Was there really a risk attached to this activity? No, apart from a bit of self-consciousness and embarrassment at the beginning.

I pushed through it, knowing it would be good for me. After the first two or three vocal warm-ups, I just wasn't self-conscious any more. (My teacher's reassuring me that I didn't sound like an animal in distress did help.) The fear about the singing lesson had been confronted and diminished. I actually enjoyed myself and partly regretted not having done it sooner, but I was glad that I had kept it – unbeknownst to myself – as a tool in the face of greater fear.

There's no correlation that I know of between singing lessons and TV interviews, but, for me, there is a strong argument to be made for knocking one fear out of the park while on the road to facing another. It proves to yourself that you can do something that you had feared. It proves that you are made of stronger stuff. It takes all of your positive thinking and affirmations and puts them into real action, which is the only way to feel truly confident. It made me feel more resilient. Taking a risk (well, a small one), and surviving, gave me a thrill. And all of that made me feel more capable of what I was about to embark upon. I would still feel incredibly nervous by the time I was sat on the couch of a morning TV show with four hundred face-melting lights in my face, but I had a strength, brought about by my previous sidestepping adventures.

Exercise
SIDESTEPPING
....

Think of a smaller fear that you've been putting off. Maybe it's something you've wanted to do but it makes you feel nervous, such as taking a dance class. Find an activity that pushes you outside of your comfort zone with little consequence and low risk and then save it for a few days before you plan to face a greater fear or challenge. When you spend a little time outside of your comfort zone and prove to yourself that you can go there, stepping back outside of it again when it comes to what counts won't be as daunting.

Tool #8 – Fear Hacking

FEAR HACKING – the perfect tool for people who roll their eyes at positive thinking.

We live in a society that favours positivity. We say, 'Don't worry, it will be fine', and we want to be seen to be glass-half-full people. If someone's not projecting positivity out into the world, we think there's something wrong with them. But have you ever found that forcing positivity makes you any less anxious or any more confident as a result? It can work, for sure – there's a whole positivity industry making millions from the very idea – but, for me, it's not always the best or the only way to deal with things effectively.

Within this positive cultural context, it's also thought that if you *think* you are going to fail or even entertain the idea of failing as a possibility, then fail you will. 'What you think, you become', etc. These positive thinkers would prefer only to visualise the best possible outcome (and they've probably read *The Secret*). But then there are those, like Elon Musk (CEO of Tesla) of whom I spoke back in the confidence chapter, who wholly embrace the idea of things going tits up, because the likelihood of that happening is sometimes very high (especially with what he's doing). But worry not, it's not as Armageddon-like as it sounds. Elon Musk refers to this as fatalism and, being naturally inclined to worry, I'm a big fan.

Instead of fatalism, I like to think of it as a psychological process of fear hacking – it just sounds a bit more proactive than fatalism. It basically involves imagining the worst-case scenario and taking the steps necessary to manage any negative eventuality. You might also call it decatastrophising or controlled catastrophic thinking. The key here is the word *controlled*. You don't want to find yourself spiralling down a rabbit hole of generalised worst-case scenarios, which will just increase your fear, so you do it in a measured way, focusing on specifics. Maybe writing it down on paper at a time when you've decided to allow for it to happen helps (think of it in the same way you might assign ten minutes a day where you are fully free to get all your worrying done). You don't want to be thinking of the worst-case scenario, such as 'I'm never going to get the job I want', from morning until night, which is the sort of thing that tends to be a major driver of anxiety.

Again, this may seem counterintuitive at first but, in small doses, there's a lot to be said for considering an outcome that doesn't go your way. Obviously, your hope is that it doesn't happen, but if it does – and sometimes it will – it makes a huge difference to have already confronted that reality and perhaps have developed a contingency plan for it.

It means you are prepared. It removes the chances of a knee-jerk, anxiety-fuelled reaction. It also diminishes the idea of the 'unknown' because you're interacting directly with your fear, which, in turn, diminishes the weight of your fear.

Think about a good horror movie. Sometimes we see someone running away from something and we don't know what it is, which makes it all the more scary. We can't see it. But when we do eventually see it (such as the weird Venus flytrap Demogorgon from *Stranger Things*), it becomes a lot less terrifying. We fear things more because we are so busy running away from them and not willing to stop and look at what it is we're actually afraid of.

By refusing to think of the worst-case scenario or turn around and confront the shadow that's chasing us down, the fear remains more exaggerated than the reality.

What's more, I find that unwavering optimism about the future only makes for a greater shock when things go wrong. In his book *The Antidote: Happiness for People Who Can't Stand Positive Thinking*, Oliver Burkeman explains that when you fight to maintain only positive thoughts about the future, you might actually find yourself less prepared, and more distressed, particularly when bad things happen, and you're unable to put a positive spin on them.[55]

Don't just focus on the sh*t *not* hitting the fan. If the sh*t does hit the fan, you *can* cope with that too. Focus on that instead.

When you get to a point of saying, 'Okay, let's be realistic, this could go horribly wrong but I'm prepared and I'm going to do it and hope for the best', the fear of failure will feel somewhat detached from you, especially if you've followed the previous step of exercising your fears so they're no longer pent up inside you.

Elon Musk says during a video interview with Sam Altman for Y Combinator: 'When starting SpaceX, I thought the odds of success were less than 10 per cent and I just accepted that, actually, probably I would just lose everything. But that maybe we would make some progress.'

The progress for you might not be a major discovery within the realm of technology (I'll leave that to Musk), but it might be progress in terms of personal development. It might be progress in terms of that which you fear not being as scary in reality.

You will have learned that sitting down and teasing your fears apart is probably one of the best ways of making the fear less exaggerated. The best way to get your fear hacking on is to first ask yourself, 'What could go wrong here?' That part should be easy to do. The next part, though, is crucial: following up these worst-case scenario questions with 'What if?', which helps you make a plan to avoid disaster. What happens if it all goes wrong? For example, what will happen to you if you finally tell that person the truth? Then what? In most cases, the worst-case scenario will feel a lot more catastrophic than it would turn out to be if it actually came true. It either won't happen, or it will and you'll survive it, or it won't be as bad as you originally feared. Furthermore, having planned for a disaster, it's likely that you'll improve your performance (regardless of the outcome) having used this strategy.

Follow your fears to the point of having a resolution if they were to come true, knowing that you can cope with all eventualities. For example: 'I'm afraid of telling my friend something that I found out that I know will hurt her. If I tell her she might be mad at me and we might argue.' Okay, and what if you do argue? It will make you feel bad but will it be permanent? What then? Will you learn something? Will you feel better for having told her the truth and done the right thing? Will your friendship eventually be the stronger for it? Will you be ready to explain to her why you had to tell her and ready for her to react unfavourably? Now, chances are that, in reality, she won't react quite as negatively as you are expecting. But by interacting with the possibility, you can plan what to do if it all goes Pete Tong. You can be okay with the risk you are taking.

This strategy applies very well to instances of public speaking. Instead of just thinking something will be an epic failure in general, which would be unhelpfully negative, I drill down into specifics. I will imagine any and all of the following worst-case scenarios:

○ I could trip over a wire
○ My slides might not work on the screen
○ I won't remember what I had wanted to say
○ I won't be able to hold my notes because I have to hold a microphone.

All of these things make me more anxious about the task at hand. Then, I go through each fear and plan for it. I bring duct tape with me to pin down any rogue wires where I'll be standing. I charge my laptop in advance and I bring my plug just in case. I write my presentation out on cue cards and I print two copies, which I bring with me. I tell the organisers in advance that I don't want to hold a microphone so they can either arrange a stand or I'll speak without one. Had I just thought to myself, 'It will all be fine', when really I had these worries, I would have turned up and experienced some of these issues, which would have been ten times worse had I not prepared in advance. And, most of all, my performance wouldn't have been as good as it could have been had I not considered the ways in which things could go wrong.

All of this is the lesser known upshot to pessimism, an unexpected tool within your confidence kit. I recommend it.

Tool #9 – Positive Visualisation

OF COURSE, there's still room for some positivity. The key, though, is to get your controlled fatalism or fear hacking out of the way first, meaning you've dealt with the negative – then the positive that's left will feel more authentic. That way, it's not forced. It's not negating your concerns, and it can have a far more beneficial impact on your confidence.

Thinking positively is something that has been practised and encouraged since the year dot. It's nothing new. Positive visualisation, however, is a little more specific and practical, so it gets my stamp of approval. It has been popular since the 1970s, particularly for athletes. Positive visualisation is the ultimate motivator; imagining how you will feel, visualising the success that you are about to embark upon. It's the best-case scenario. But it's more than just thinking about the end result and it requires effort. It actually pays to imagine yourself as the confident person you want to be, the person who is unfazed by self-consciousness, the person who gets the job done (be it performing in a match, socialising at a party with ease, passing a test with flying colours and maybe even enjoying the process or giving the most engaging and thought-provoking speech of your life) – it's for wherever in your life you need the confidence boost most.

Several studies on mental imagery have shown that our brains can't really tell the difference between a picture that is real and a picture that we are imagining – this is why you'll feel scared when you think of something scary, even if there's nothing scary right in front of you. The same chemicals are released and the same neural pathways (which link what your body does to the brain impulses that control it) are activated. This is conditioning (which we covered in Chapter 2) and it makes sense that this could work in our favour too. One of the better-known stories is that of golfer Jack Nicklaus, who practised each shot in his mind before taking it and believed it to be a huge part of his success.

When we repeat a thought over time, it can become a belief and can have the same power as actions. We know this to be true from Cognitive Behavioural Therapy. But I find it works best in terms of confidence when you've already dealt with your fears and concerns, when you're not just trying to shove a positive mental image in and squish down all of your worries so they can't breathe and might, at any moment, explode. That's not what we want. Instead, we confront the negatives and then we get on to this more positive mental exercise, which should then be followed up with physical action if it's to prove beneficial.

Positive visualisation, which should engage as many senses as you can, gets you that bit closer to realising your goals. Muhammad Ali was a big fan of immersing himself, through mental imagery, in every second of a fight before he went into the ring. He would imagine it going well, imagine the perfect punches he would throw. (Positive self-affirmations such as 'I am the greatest', which Ali became famous for, also helped.)

When you make it a regular practice, this mental exercise enhances your motivation, it primes your brain for success, your brain is already practising the task at hand and therefore learning how best to do it. Studies have even shown that it can improve motor performance when it's eventually crunch time. By imagining ourselves as calm and competent, we reduce the physiological symptoms of stress. By practising what we're about to do in our heads, and doing it several times, it is believed that you can condition your neural pathways in such a way that by the time you go to actually do it, the action is familiar to your brain. And that which is familiar doesn't bring about a fear response (at least not to the same extent as something that is totally unknown).

How to do it?

1. Recall a confident memory

I find some classical conditioning of your own can be a helpful place to start. Close your eyes and think back to a time when you were really confident or did something really well or felt really chuffed with yourself. Bring it right into your focus – what can you see? What did you feel? What were you wearing? Who was there? What can you touch? What were you thinking? Talk through it in your head or tell someone about it until you feel as though you're back there. Pinch your forefinger and your thumb together, eyes still closed. When you repeat this a few times, it creates a link between the imagery in your head and the physical act of pinching your fingers together. Then, when you most need to muster that confidence later on, holding your fingers in this way will more easily take you back to that feeling of confidence. This is called anchoring and is a widely used technique among public speakers.

2. Employ relaxation techniques

Next, you need to visualise the task at hand. Remember that you've already given plenty of energy to all of the things that could go wrong, so now your focus is purely imagining things going in your favour. Sit with your back straight and breathe in through your nose and out through your mouth for as long as it takes for you to feel somewhat relaxed. It helps too if you count down from ten very slowly, and with each number, you go down a step on a staircase (this is one thing I found useful from a hypnotherapy session, at least in terms of reaching that initial point of relaxation).

3. Don't just visualise, engage as many senses as you can

Next, bring the future scene into your mind's eye. What can you see? What can you touch? What can you smell? What outcome do you want? How do you see yourself? How do you see your body language? How are people responding to you? How are you speaking? How are you holding yourself? What are your strengths in this situation? Try to bring as much detail into the mental image as possible. What you are feeling as you do it and as you achieve the result you want is key, as is visualising yourself as you will be in the real situation, and not as someone else observing you.

4. Practise it again and again

Remember to keep it realistic, this exercise is not about

imagining yourself as a millionaire and waking up as one tomorrow. As explained by Tom Seabourne PhD, an athlete and imagery expert and the author of *The Complete Idiot's Guide To Quick Total Body Workouts*, positive imagery 'can't make you perform beyond your capabilities, but it can help you reach your potential'.[56]

Tool #10 – Preparation, Experience, Repetition

WHEN ALL OTHER tools have been employed, all that's left is the hard work itself. Remember, you can read about confidence all you want, but until you take things into your own hands, you'll only get so far.

This is a three-part tool which will take you over the finish line. First you prepare - let's call this 'hedging' - then you experience it and then you repeat it (if it's something that can be repeated) until that which was outside of your comfort zone is now within it.

1. Preparation

To me, preparation is essential, and though it might sound obvious to you as well, preparation (or a lack thereof) is the biggest determinant of whether or not something works out. Doing whatever you can to hedge things (which is to reduce or mitigate your risks) is the holy grail of confidence tools. If you're an anxious person and you experience the fear of failure as acutely as I have done, there's no such thing as being over-prepared, and there should be no 'winging it', until it's something you are very comfortable with.

In a previous job, I had the opportunity to interview countless movie stars in London. Needless to say, for the first few, I couldn't eat for two days beforehand on account of the fear of f*cking it up. I was warned about overdoing it on preparation and going in with every sentence in my head planned out because it almost never goes exactly how you would think, but the only way I could feel like it was something I could face was if I covered my arse for every eventuality.

I'd only have maybe five minutes max with the actor, but I was going to equip myself with enough knowledge as possible so that nothing could throw me off-guard. I didn't just want to get through it without projectile vomiting into their face, I wanted to do a really good job. Spending a good few hours researching their previous work and their forthcoming work, and watching them in other similar interviews not only helped me perform better in my own interview, but it took a lot of the fear of the unknown out of the equation.

Preparation gives you the best chance of success. Preparation is something you can control, it can get you as close as possible to achieving what it is you want to achieve, and then the rest, which you cannot control, is up to fate. Again, this will all sound like common sense, but sometimes when we feel the fear of failure so strongly, we decide to just not deal with it and 'see what happens'.

I can assure you, the chances of things going your way when you're winging it are slim. And the chances of feeling absolutely petrified, when you're about to take to the podium and you haven't prepared, are high. Hedging is my most reliable armour against the fear of failure. Preparation gives you a head start on success.

2. Experience
The second part of this tool involves taking the action we've been talking about all along. Pursuing the goal, taking the specific steps required to reach the goal – whatever that may be. This is where you enter the learning zone. You've left the comfort zone, you've prepared and engaged all of the other tools to get you

this far, now you have to do it. This is what we fear the most, but having done all of that previous work, you'll now know that most of the fear of failure is wrapped up in anticipation. Waiting for action is what gets me more than anything. When the time comes around to do your thing, you're as ready as you'll ever be.

You do it, you experience it, and it goes well or it goes not so well. Either way, you've learned something. What not to do, what to do next time, what works for you, that you are stronger than you thought – the list of insights goes on, provided you're prepared to accept any outcome as a source of feedback. Jump to Part Three for more on this.

3. Repetition

The final part of this tool is, again, action-based. It is repetition – or you could call it practice. You repeat the thing that scares you, or things that are similar to it, until the boundaries of your comfort zone are stretched to include this new experience. Most often, what we really fear is failing to get something right the first time. So you do it again. What's more, our fear of failure is often short-sighted. We don't fear failing at something after years of practice. And we never fear it as much after the first time. So you do it again, whether it was a good experience or whether you perceived it as a failure. It probably wasn't until I had done about ten film interviews that I stopped having cramps in the days leading up to one. After that, I would only feel nervous right before the interview began, and I was okay with that fear because I knew it would help me perform better and bring my 'A' game. I didn't expect to ever be fear free. But I wasn't afraid of failing.

Repetition enables you to build, slowly but surely, on the initial confidence you gain from an experience. It gives you a chance to try different things. Maybe for you, it was a social experiment. With a lack of confidence about socialising with people you don't know, you went to an event on your own to stretch your comfort zone. After the first initial experience, you will have new learnings to put into action the second and third time.

In Cognitive Behavioural Therapy, this is known as exposure therapy, and it's what we do when we are trying to extinguish a fear. If you have a bad experience and you run away, you'll confirm the belief in your head that your fears were right and you shouldn't have done it. You will keep the fear conditioning in place. If you expose yourself to it again and again, and see that all of your worst fears are not realised and the risks are lowered, the fear diminishes while your confidence grows. Even for the most confident and self-assured people in the world who take on something for the first time – it can take several goes before they get it right, let alone get good at it. Then, when it comes to testing yourself in other areas, having seen how repetition can help you, you will realise that it's just not realistic to expect yourself to get everything right the first time. And you might just give yourself a break.

But even repeating something again and again won't eliminate the fear entirely, but it does diminish it. It puts things in perspective when you realise that, in half an hour, the talk or the interview or whatever it was you feared will be over and life will go on.

It's not easy. When you're really struggling with fear, these last steps can be enough to make you close this book and binge-watch *Friends* instead. But your self-confidence will only increase when you do the work involved in preparation, you do the work involved by taking action (instead of just thinking about it) and you do your homework by repeating it. It will only increase when you do the work and take action. (Yes, it bears repeating for emphasis.)

Tool #11 – How To Fake It Till You Make It

SOMETIMES, when you're nervous or so unsure of yourself that you forget your own name, the suggestion of faking it till you make it seems downright delusional. But whatever you think, this is a concept based on a series of actions that has been backed up by countless studies, so, if nothing else, it can't do any harm.

Ultimately, we want to manage our emotions and learn to do stuff that scares us while feeling calm (so that there is less need to fake it), but faking it until you make it can work for a while and can certainly lead to actually making it.

Here's what I do when I'm trying to convince myself that I am a pro. Essentially, it's a courage recipe (and courage is what steps in when confidence is absent).

1. Smile

Granted, this is one you might curl your lip at – I would – but smiling reduces stress, and when we reduce stress we increase feelings of confidence. A quirky but no less worthy 2012 study in *Psychological Science* took 169 students and trained them to hold chopsticks in their mouths.[57] When held in certain ways, one group were mimicking a standard smile, another group were left neutral, and another group were smiling genuinely (which involves engaged eye muscles as well as mouth muscles). They were then asked to carry out difficult cognitive tasks, all the while holding the smiling positions. Interestingly, not just those with genuine smiles but also those with the standard forced smiles had a much lower heart rate than those with a neutral expression. Fake smiles count.

2. Change my body language

Stand up or sit up tall with your shoulders back and your chest out. Do not hunch over and cross your arms or try to resemble Gollum from *The Lord of the Rings* in any way – think Mufasa from *The Lion King* instead. Hold yourself in this position for two minutes (or adopt this kind of pose as much as you can throughout the day).

This goes back to Harvard psychologist Amy Cuddy's research that demonstrates the power of body language in boosting confidence.[58] She writes: 'Our nonverbals govern how we think and feel about ourselves. Our bodies change our minds.' And she went to Harvard so I'm not going to argue with that. Foetal position be gone!

3. Get dressed

I get out of my PJs or my comfy clothes and I get into the kind of clothes I'd wear when I mean business. This is one of the oldest tricks in the book – dressing for the job you want. It might sound trivial but just think about the boost of confidence you feel when you think you look good (whether it's for an important day or not). You feel better about yourself. I do my hair and makeup and dress myself so that I feel as good as I can. Yes, it's what's on the inside that truly counts, but feeling good about how you're presented to the world has a positive, knock-on effect to your confidence. I even feel this if I merely get dressed up and sit at home with my dog.

And, yep, there was a study for this one too, from North-western University in the US.[59] Participants were divided into three groups: the first group was asked to put on a white lab coat and the second a painter's coat (which to my mind is pretty much the same as the lab coat but with paint splashes on it?) while the third group were left as they were but were shown a lab coat. They were each then given an exercise that involved examining four sets of two pictures for differences, which tested how well they could sustain attention. The group in the lab coats found more differences in half the time of those in the artist's coats (they were all equally as competent), which led the researchers to believe that it wasn't just about what they were wearing, but the symbolic meaning of what they were wearing. So don't just dress up as a clown; dress appropriately for the task at hand. In fact, I'm going to get changed right now into my I'm-a-serious-writer ensemble and enjoy writing this brief guide an awful lot more.

4. Act like you're qualified, even if you don't feel that you are

This one's hard, and you get better at it, but it's so effective. I take a deep breath and I walk into a room and introduce myself, shake hands, smile, make small talk and remind myself that I'm here for a reason. Either I am good enough or somebody here thinks I am good enough. I act as though I believe in myself and by acting that way, I start to believe it.

5. Watch your language

This is another very hard one that won't vanish overnight for you, but it's very easy to speak in a way that sounds apologetic when you're nervous or lacking in confidence, when you have absolutely nothing to apologise for. This happens a lot over email, and as a freelancer I find myself in this pickle every single month. So I'm chasing invoices, asking politely to be paid and it almost feels instinctive to open an email about money with an apology: 'I'm just checking in to see if you received my invoice okay' or I might even want to say 'I'm sorry to hassle you but ...' When I copped it, I made a decision to remove the word 'just' and 'sorry' from all professional correspondence where it wasn't totally necessary. Using this kind of language, I was undermining myself and opening myself up to be undermined by others or not taken seriously. And if you're not taken seriously, it's hard to feel confident. Now, when I read an email that I've written that doesn't come across as though I am too soft (while at the same time being friendly), I feel more confident in myself as a professional because I sound more confident to others. It's a game-changer.

6. Ask questions

Such as 'I'd love to know more about ...' This one's situational but it's another keeper. The tendency to stay quiet when we're unsure of ourselves is normal, but here's a better idea: deflect onto someone else. I always go into a nerve-racking situation with one or two questions that I can ask to take the heat off me. For example, if it's a job interview, ask them to tell you about the office culture. If nothing more, it gives me a minute to gather myself together. It enables me to still contribute and be heard without being put under the spotlight and it even makes it appear that I'm in control and, perhaps, even leading the conversation. Then when it's my time to shine, I feel somewhat warmed up. Keep this one to yourself though or it won't work for you.

7. Lastly, if you have something coming up that you would like to feel more confident about, make sure you build in time to do something you're really good at

In my experience, when you exercise your genuine confidence in one area, it spills over into other areas, giving you a short-term boost for whatever you're about to take on. Think of it like the turbo-boost button in Nintendo's *Mario Kart*. This could be going to the gym or doing some yoga at home (which also takes my mind away from the stress and nerves) or it could even be cooking myself some food (and I'd stick to a meal I could whip up in my sleep, instead of that time I tried something creative and set the pan on fire; a confidence-booster that is *not*).

Bonus tip

This one's from Mark Tyrrell's online resource 'Uncommon Knowledge' (which is super helpful). He says people report feeling calmer when they chew gum (I can't right now because I have braces and that would definitely be stress-inducing). 'Chewing gum produces saliva, meaning it's time to eat (as far as the instincts are concerned), and if it's okay to eat then there can't be a real threat in the environment so other stress mechanisms tend to "stand down". Really what helps is anything that we wouldn't do in a life or death situation – such as standing around and talking or smiling. This gives the feedback to the "emergency services" that all that investment in stress energy isn't really needed after all.'[60]

If you're still in doubt about faking it till you make it, consider this nugget. According to Jeff Wise in an article for *Psychology Today*, several studies have shown that contrary to what we might expect, we don't actually peer inwards when it comes to creating beliefs about ourselves.[61] We don't decide that we are confident or not confident in this way. Instead, we look precisely at how we're behaving and acting to the outside world. We observe our own external behaviour as opposed to our internal monologue. And if our external behaviour takes the shape of a confident, self-assured person, we start to develop and confirm this belief about ourselves. He says: 'If we see ourselves carrying out a particular action, our self-conception molds itself to explain that reality.'

In other words, behave like the person you want to become on the outside and allow how you feel on the inside to follow suit. It will.

Tool #12 – The Night Gremlins

YOU MAY HAVE noticed that when we're anxiously anticipating a particular event or are feeling very concerned about something specific, we feel it more at night. It's not about being afraid of the dark (okay sometimes that still gets me), our worries just come out when we're tired, like gremlins. I've always found that I'm more vulnerable at the time when my body craves rest. This can be so off-putting and make things feel far more catastrophic than they would in the light of day. I wanted to include a quick guide for dealing with those dark-hour demons.

Having trouble drifting off is one thing. It's very disconcerting to be jolted awake with worry when you've already been asleep. This is another evolutionary feature; though you might not be aware of it, we sleep in cycles of ninety minutes to two hours. We wake up regularly, move our position in the bed and go into the next stage of sleep. If we're relatively worry-free, we rarely notice this. The reason we've evolved to wake up every so often is to check for danger. When predatory animals were a threat at night, we'd wake up on high alert. Now, we've replaced the predatory animals with more contemporary stresses. So if we're feeling particularly worried about something, when we do switch from those states of sleeping, our brains will bring those worries right to our attention. Sometimes, we can even find ourselves consumed with dread about things we didn't think we were even worried about. Cheers, evolution.

It's important to understand that, at night, our worries can multiply simply because we have the additional stress of not being able to get to sleep. Now, not only are you worried about what it is you're worried about, but you also worry about the fact that you should be asleep and so you'll probably feel the effects of this tomorrow.

In her book *Tired But Wired: How To Overcome Your Sleep Problems*, Dr Nerina Ramlakhan explains that our conscious minds are very active during the day, focusing on the tasks we need to complete, but when we fall asleep at night, our barriers come down and the subconscious mind takes over. So any worries that might have been lurking during the day come up to the surface and, in our sleepy state, they're magnified beyond reality.

She calls these thoughts 'gremlins', and sometimes that's exactly what they feel like.[62] Interestingly, certain personality types will feel it more. For example, people who are creative, emotionally sensitive or very empathetic (I feel a great deal of empathy for pigeons, for example, whereas someone else might describe them as 'rats of the sky') are more likely than others to experience issues with sleep.

This biological mishap has inspired many a night-terror movie.

1. Don't take them seriously

Above all else, take all of your worries at night with a pinch of salt. You don't have to try really hard not to panic or feel afraid, because that will just make you feel it more, but say, 'Okay, I'm feeling this way now, I'm going to see how I feel in the morning,' Accept it. Don't try to resist it.

2. Don't engage with bright screens

Don't pick up the phone to scroll online or check the time. Instead, I find a simple breathing exercise helps to keep me relaxed. Breathe in for four and breathe out for eight. This slows your heart rate. Focus on the in and out breath as much as you can and it will become very soothing.

Sometimes, I even add the mouthing of a word to this exercise. For instance. I might mouth the word 'rest' in the out breath. The only reason I do this is because it's really boring and I get bored and tired of doing it so I usually fall asleep after a while.

3. Rest is good for you, even if you're not asleep

This is not new advice, but worrying about falling back asleep is never going to help you drift off again. Whether she's right or not, my mother always told me that if we're awake, it's okay. Rest is still good for our body even if we're not asleep. So if I find myself staring at the ceiling panicked about something, this at least takes the sleep stress out of the equation. I'll still benefit from resting and focusing on my breathing.

4. Sleep on it

If I've opted in to something that scares me, at night I'll want desperately to back-track. Don't make any decisions or judgements in the middle of the night. Even if it feels like your gut is telling you something, wait until the morning.

5. Schedule a worry period

If there's something on the horizon that you're consciously fearful of or stressed out about, give yourself some worry time maybe an hour before you go to bed. Try to exercise all of your worries out of you and let your mind go to the worst-case scenarios. Often, when you've already addressed it consciously, your subconscious doesn't feel the need to throw it back up at you in the middle of the night. Worry periods might seem counterintuitive but they have proven very useful for lots of chronic worriers. Having turned it into a task, when you're outside of your worry period, you don't feel the need as much.

6. Get up for a few minutes

If you're finding it particularly difficult, just remove yourself from the situation for a bit. Sit on the couch and read something (that isn't related to your worries) and then come back to bed in twenty minutes or so. This isn't giving in to the worry, it's taking action.

PART THREE

FINAL TOOLS

What To Do
When You Fail

YOU FAILED. What now?

Everything you've read thus far helps you get to the point of taking action. In a way, if you've got here, you've already overcome your fear of failure, which is so heavily wrapped up in the anticipation of the event. But say you do go all in, you give it your best shot and it doesn't work out. What if things go epically wrong? What if your initial fears are confirmed and you're left thinking: 'I knew it. I was right not to want to try this'? At this point, the failing part doesn't really matter. How you react in the face of it is what counts.

I'm not about to fill you full of 'silver linings' waffle – we have Pinterest for that. Let's just be honest: most of the time, when you don't win or achieve or have something go well, especially something that you've really wanted and worked very hard to get, you feel beat down, worn out, negative, frustrated, disappointed, sad, sometimes regretful and generally like a sack of miserable potatoes. If you're as motivated as I would be when I set my mind to something, this state of mind is unavoidable. When people say, 'Well, wasn't it nice to be nominated anyway?' or 'It's not about winning, it's about taking part' or 'You live and learn', you want to punch them in the face (though for the last one, they have a point). At the very least, you want to roll your eyes and have yourself a little pity party.

That's okay.

Do it.

Allow yourself a little time to wallow and feel like crap. Don't force yourself to be all smiles through gritted teeth. If you've worked hard, you are entitled to feel disappointed and, as with all negative emotions, burying those feelings will only cause them to bubble up later on. But remember it's a state of mind that can change, if you want it to.

I'm not expecting that you'll suddenly *like* the taste of failure, but when you're ready, allow yourself to learn from it. In the face of failure – whatever that might be to you – expect and allow for these hard-to-swallow emotions and also expect that you're probably going to beat yourself up about it for a little while – but then STOP. Put a time limit on this. Process the setback and then shift your thinking proactively towards learning.

If you have to take out a pen and paper to convince yourself, do it. Failure is hard because, in most circumstances, it causes us to look at ourselves and accept that maybe we didn't know as much as we thought or maybe we weren't ready for it or maybe we misjudged things, or maybe we're not perfect (well, we're *not*, and this shouldn't come as breaking news, but I wonder when we – myself included – will stop being surprised by this fact). But failure is not a permanent fixture. It's a temporary blow to our self-confidence and when we decide to learn from it, it's a blow that heals more strongly. Think of the pain you feel after a good workout. Your weaker muscles tear – hence the short-term pain – and then they quickly repair to be so much stronger, meaning you can now handle more weight or go further than you first expected.

Nelson Mandela said: 'I either win or I learn', and it's a mantra worth tattooing on your brain.

Though those negative emotions are first to arrive in the face of failure – thank you, limbic brain – that's not to say they're right. When your rational, thinking brain steps in

– when your emotive reaction is out of the way, of course – you have a clearer sense of perspective that enables you to be more accepting of the truth about failure.

What is this truth, you ask?

Ultimately, that there *is* no failure, only feedback (should you choose to take it on board). If you don't win or succeed, you learn what *not* to do. You learn quickly what *didn't* work. You are given a clear roadmap towards that which needs a little work or improvement. You learn where your strengths are and you refocus your energy around those strengths. You learn what to do next time. Because a negative experience weighs more heavily on the brain – remember our innate negativity bias? – we actually come away with crystal-clear learnings, more so than we would if we breezed right through.

This is a more healthy perception of failure that you need to get comfortable with. To think failure means something was a waste of your time is natural, but it's wrong. There is always something to learn, if you're willing. Failure can never be a waste of your time or energy, in fact it can fast track you to success the next time. Think about a significant mistake you or someone you know has made in the past. Maybe you misjudged something, maybe you thought someone would react differently than they did, maybe you thought it would be a lot easier than it was – whatever happened, you've said to yourself or to that person, 'Well, you'll certainly never make the same mistake again.' This is true, and it rings so much louder in our heads because of our brush with failure (negative emotion), which means we are even more equipped to face a similar situation in the future – and this time, we know better.

What this more appropriate perception of failure requires is a careful balance of humility and self-compassion. On one hand, you have to be able and willing to accept that you are human and imperfect and that you have much to learn. If you consistently see failure as everybody else's fault and never yours, you won't learn from it and you'll consistently come up against the same roadblocks. We all know someone who thinks the world is against them and won't accept responsibility for their actions, or lack thereof. An example of this would be consistently failing a test and blaming the material and choosing to overlook the fact that you didn't study. This attitude will cause you only to consistently come up against roadblocks.

On the other end of the spectrum, no learning can occur if you're too busy berating yourself and labelling yourself as a permanent failure. You need to go easier on yourself and accept that you gave it your best shot. And then look for those learnings.

These are two extremes, neither of which can serve us very well. I tend to lean heavily in the direction of the latter – in fact, I blame myself in situations that don't even have anything to do with me. I've had so many experiences where somebody in the same room as me is in a foul humour for whatever reason. Instantly, an avalanche of self-doubt erupts in my head as I think of all the ways in which I *must* be to blame. Maybe this person has something entirely different going on in their mind, which is almost always the case, but I'm sitting there thinking I've done something wrong. I need to ease up on this, obviously, because it is batsh*t crazy. If I berate myself in this kind of situation, you can safely assume that I wouldn't go too easy on myself if I was directly involved in some form of failure. No siree. In the past, I've been my own worst enemy, and sometimes this tendency to beat myself up can creep back in, but I'm starting to consciously embrace this more realistic and helpful perception of failure.

Here's a quick what-to-do-if-you-fail worksheet, should you find yourself in the wake of something that's gone tits up. It's based on my own experience and experimentation.

1 Firstly, exorcise your frustrations and disappointments right out of you. No priest required, just allow yourself to feel it for a while and let it all out.

2 When you've had a rant or sobbed or whatever it is you need to do to let off some steam, STOP.

3 Take out a pen and paper and rationally debrief the perceived failure you face by asking yourself the following questions:
   • What went wrong?
   • Was it within my control?
   • Was I underprepared?
   • What did I learn?
   • What would I do next time?
   • What wouldn't I do next time?
   • What do I know now that I didn't before?

4 When you've processed the constructive feedback and have a sense of what you've learned, look for partial successes, no matter how small. List as many partial successes as you can find (e.g. 'I consider it a partial success that I was brave enough to do it, even if it didn't work out' or 'I am now more confident about what I need to do next time').

5 Remind yourself of the importance and significance of failure in a person's life. If you went through life without experiencing failure, you wouldn't learn or grow; in fact you wouldn't really be living at all. As Richard Templar said, 'Only dead fish swim with the stream.' Know that you are alive and kicking and, because of this, you will sometimes have to swim upstream, against currents and other obstacles, and this is just another one of them.

6 Remind yourself of how you measure your own self-worth and your values. If you see failure as proof of your inadequacy, you need to go back to Chapter 5 and do some more work on how you view yourself.

7 Accept it. Don't see it as a roadblock, but, rather, as a building block. Where will this take you next?

8 Know that you won't make the same mistakes again. This could only happen if you were unwilling to assess the situation.

9 Replace all 'shoulds' with 'coulds' (more on this below).

10 Finally, accept that you did your best and that that is all you can ever do. If doing your best is your goal, then there is no failure.

When all that work is done, the most important thing to watch is your willingness to try again. It might not be the same thing that you get another shot at, but there will be another opportunity to try in some other capacity at some point in the near future. If you let this temporary blip set you back, you shrink your comfort zone back a level or two and that's not helpful after all of the work you've done. Cheesy though it may feel, when you come up against a brick wall or you've been beavering away only to fall down a massive snake (Snakes and Ladders board game, anyone?) that feels as though you're right back at square one, it helps to look at those in the public eye – Richard Branson, Michael Jordan to name but two – who failed time and time again before they got their break (and continued to make mistakes afterwards too). Despite being glorified by the media, these are not superhuman individuals. A certain amount of talent or competence will only get you so far; the tenacity to keep getting back up on your feet in the face of adversity is what these people have in common. Their confidence far outweighs their competence and where one person might take failure as a sign to stop and pursue something else, these guys used it as the ultimate motivation.

Imagine how much sweeter it must have been for Michael Jordan to finally join rank among the NBA's biggest stars, and earn the title as the greatest basketball player of all time, after having been kicked off his high-school team for not being good enough. Had it all been easy, he would never have appreciated it or enjoyed the success quite as much.

My 'failure'

One of the most significant experiences like this in my life so far was the decision to leave one job for another in 2014 – a move that kick-started the chain of events that led me right here.

I was very happy in my job, but I felt I had reached the ceiling in terms of progress. While I could have enjoyed where I was for a while, I felt it was important to keep pushing myself from one challenge to the next, otherwise I was afraid I might stagnate. So I took a job at a start-up company that I thought would be the best thing for me, even though I had my doubts deep down that I chose to ignore.

Long story short, it was not the right move. Now, I know that we all experience the 'Oh sh*t, have I done the right thing?' moment in our first few weeks at a new job – change is difficult most of the time – but trust me when I say I just *knew* – the way you know about a good melon (that's a quote from *When Harry Met Sally* by the way) – that this was a bad decision within the first few hours of day one.

It wasn't the place or the people or the job itself – it just wasn't right for me and I was instantly filled with fear and regret. What had I done? Why didn't I listen to my gut that was saying no? Whatever happened, I was here now. I couldn't retrace my steps. My old job had been filled, I'd said yes to this one and signed contracts and the wheels were already in motion. I had to give it a shot to the best of my ability, but every fibre of my being wanted to run. I couldn't stomach conversations about company plans for the next year let alone the next five years.

My body was there but my mind wasn't and it made me very sick and very anxious. I ignored it again because I couldn't admit to myself or those around me that I'd made a mistake – the 'failure' – and so the stress built up and up until I was suffering with full-blown, crippling anxiety, the kind that would eventually keep me housebound, unemployed and getting through each day from one violent panic attack to the next.

Because I became so ill and so gripped by anxiety, I blamed myself enormously for making this job change. I used language on a daily basis such as 'I should never have left', 'I should have known this would happen' and I dwelled heavily on the past. I was also petrified about the future. What had I done?

Now for me at the time, it wasn't as simple as filling out this worksheet and being on my merry way; it took me a long, long time to accept that life had just worked out this way and that I'd have to deal with the consequences of my decision and to stop holding myself ransom for one misjudged move. It took me even longer to look for the partial successes and the learnings and to accept that maybe things had worked out this way for a reason. Eventually, when I got on top of the anxiety – which is detailed in *Owning It* – I was able to reframe how I looked at this life event.

Instead of seeing it as a failure or a black ink stain on the story of my life, which it certainly felt like, I now look back on this time as a massive learning curve. I gained invaluable insights that have shaped the person I am today. So let's look back with kinder eyes: I made the best decision I could at the time with the information I had. I was brave to take a leap into the unknown, but not every leap will work out and there is the risk of failure in everything we do.

I learned that my body will tell me if it's not happy with something and that maybe I should trust my instincts when they're roaring at me. Though this life manoeuvre made me feel temporarily weak – 'Why can't I just get on with things like everyone else?' – I learned that I am far more resilient than I would ever have given myself credit for. I wouldn't have known this about myself if I didn't get through that experience. And I got through it.

Because I felt such fear at that time – fear that I had done irreparable damage to myself and I might never be well again – I was able to test my bravery. I learned that I could get through a very difficult time and come out the better for it. I learned to appreciate that I am sensitive instead of berating myself for it. I learned that I'm not the kind of person who will thrive when working crazy long hours, and that is okay. I had a rude awakening that being well matters in my life more than any job opportunity. Because I was willing to rectify the situation, no matter how long it took (and it took me a few years), I was confident that I would never wind up in the same scenario again. I now knew what to do if something similar presented itself. I had been there and done that and, ultimately, I had experience, which can never be a bad thing.

I took what I perceived to be a major roadblock and got right on top of it – it was now a building block, restructuring my life to benefit from what I had learned.

Shoulds and coulds: the importance of language

Most of all, I was able to change my wording from 'should/ should not' to 'could', or other less severe responses. Instead of saying, 'I shouldn't have taken that job', I said, 'Well, it's happened and I can't change that but I could take this experience and turn it to something positive.' And that was my first book.

It might seem insignificant or all about semantics but 'should' is really negative. The language we use with ourselves is hugely important. According to Dr Shad Helmstetter in his book *What To Say When You Talk To Your Self*, 'should' is chastisement. When we use the word *should* there's an unsaid follow up that says 'but I'm not'. It's just more of that beating yourself over the head with a frying pan that will never do you any good. 'I should have this book written by now', 'I should be at the gym'. 'Could', on the other hand, opens up opportunity for the future; it's kinder, more compassionate and more fair. It offers a suggestion or an invitation to ourselves instead of slamming a definitive 'should' in our faces, which does nothing more than reinforce negative behaviour and negative beliefs about ourselves.

Tell yourself now, 'I should be making more money.' This sentence inherently blames you for the fact that you're not and alludes to some assumed incompetency. Now say, 'I could make more money' or 'I'd like to make more money. How can I do that?' This language has an entirely different message. This makes you think of opportunity. This is positive and suggests that you absolutely have it within you to achieve what you want. It makes you think proactively about how to get there instead of wallowing in the fact that you're not there right now. It's inspiring, whereas 'should' is damning.

See what I mean?

When was the last time you said you should do more or be more and, as a result, you did more or became more? Doesn't work for me. When we use the word 'should', we're automatically denying our current situation – for example, 'I shouldn't have said that'; well, I did, so what can I do about it now? With 'should', we're not accepting of where we are, nor are we ready to move forward, and if we're not accepting, we're definitely not moving. Instead of language that confirms a lack of self-acceptance or self-belief, use language that encourages you.

In this way, when we reframe our self-talk, we reframe our experience.

What To Do When You Succeed

SO YOU'VE DONE IT and you've nailed it. Success! What now?

1 Okay. First of all, take a f*cking minute. Please.
2 Pour yourself a hefty glass of praise and ...
3 Do not be so quick to discard your achievements.

This is IMPORTANT – so important, I used all caps.

Something we tend to overlook with such ease is how to handle and appreciate success, the very thing we strive for. And if we make a balls of this part, what was the point of all that personal development and hard work in the first place?

This gets so little of our energy when you consider how much time we spend worrying and getting there in

271

advance, which is why I'm giving it pride of place in its own chapter.

Think about it. We always ask so many questions about failure and how to *achieve* success but we know so little of what to do when it's finally there in our lap. Of failure, we ask how to avoid it, how to stomach it, how to grow from it, how to get past it; we want to be better equipped in every sense with failure. But for a good many of us, we're ill-equipped to embrace success. Some people refer to it as a 'fear of success', but I see it more as a 'whatever' attitude to success when we eventually get it.

For the most part, we don't give a second thought to success (when it's been achieved, that is), when this is what we've yearned for all along. Think about the last time you passed with flying colours or rose to the challenge, whatever that may have been. As is common to so many of us, by the time we've achieved what we set out to achieve, we've already moved on to the next thing. It's like we instantly dispose of our rear-view mirror because we need only look ahead. We might say, 'Oh, that's great' – we might even pop some champers for a particular triumph – but then we just get used to it. The dust settles and it does so quickly and we're already looking ahead. We get the promotion today and by tomorrow, it's yesterday's news.

Why does this happen?

There are a few reasons. For starters, we adapt to the win and it becomes our new norm; our perception of how hard it was or how significant it was changes. This is a very natural reaction and it would happen if you won the lottery too. Whatever happens in life, and wherever you find yourself on the wealth spectrum, we all have a level of relative equilibrium that we return to; everything else is a temporary peak or trough - and if you don't want to take my word for it, watch the documentary *Happy* (a movie and a movement). Our adaptive nature is one of the defining characteristics of being human and because of that, seemingly insurmountable challenges can become doable. We climb to the top of the proverbial mountain with all our might only to look down and find that it's just a hill; we could do it in less than half the time now. If there's a challenge involved, you can consider this a successful expansion of your comfort zone in that you no longer perceive the task in the same negative or fearful or enormous way. While this is a good thing - there's an unhelpful side-effect: we can belittle and - well, there's just no nicer way to say this - essentially piss all over what we've achieved.

When our perception changes and shrinks that mountain down to a hill and we forget how we used to feel, it now feels like no big deal, and if it's no big deal, we struggle to appreciate it. We have to make ourselves appreciate it.

If that sounds familiar, worry not; I'm guilty of this too and I know a good many people who would be the same. Rarely do we take the time to analyse and appreciate our success in the same way we would sit back and mull over a perceived failure. But we should replace the latter with the former. We need to consciously tilt the scales back in favour of the positive (because remember, we are always grappling with our innate negativity bias). For me, this nonchalant attitude to success is hugely disproportionate to the weight of the fear of failure that preceded it. So much so, that the lack of appreciation for getting it right every now and then makes you question why you worried so much or worked so hard in the first place. What's the point if we're going to immediately disregard our efforts?

With success, we can get what I consider to be the opposite of rose-tinted glasses, looking back on our achievements with a well-that-was-nothing attitude when we should really stop and remind ourselves of how far we've come or what it took to get here. Once achieved, it's very easy to take accomplishments for granted, and if this is your modus operandi, is there any value in success at all?

Now let's talk about self-praise, a necessary ingredient for handling success.

> 'You're, like, really pretty.'
> 'Thank you!'
> 'So you agree?'
> 'What?'
> 'You think you're really pretty.'
> *Mean Girls* (2004)

Something we also need to be mindful of – and perhaps it's more of an Irish thing and from what I've read it's definitely a female thing – is our unquestionable allergy to self-praise (or any praise, for that matter), which puts a major roadblock in front of our appreciation of our achievements. This is not me being dramatic, it's a goddamn epidemic. We're not just mildly intolerant of speaking kindly about ourselves, we're full-blown *allergic*. This is pretty significant because, as you know, how we talk to ourselves and about ourselves to others impacts hugely on our experience, our confidence and our chances of success.

Why do we find it so easy to approve of other people's achievements but not our own?

We're conditioned to be humble and enormously self-deprecating. In fact, it's almost seen as rude or arrogant to think highly of yourself (*Mean Girls* explores this better than I could articulate here) and this is one social construct that does nothing but hinder us. Humility is favourable in most societies and bragging is not. Socially, we may come across as more down to earth and likeable to others, but to what end? The more you refuse to take a compliment or appreciate and accept one of your own achievements, the more you begin to unravel the confidence you've been cultivating thus far. So stop. Can we just all agree that to pat yourself on the back doesn't have to mean you think the sun shines out of your arse?

And so what if you do think that?

If you read as many personal development books as I do, one thing they all have in common is that we'd probably be a lot happier if we *did* believe the sun shone out of there.

Now you don't have to grab a megaphone and start telling the world how amazing you are, it can be done quietly. Really all that matters is you tell it to yourself. And more than that, that you start to believe it. This is not egotistical or selfish, so beat those conditioned thoughts right out of your head.

In *Brag: The Art of Tooting Your Own Horn Without Blowing It*, author Peggy Klaus explains that although self-promotion is crucial for career growth, many professionals simply find it too difficult: 'So ingrained are the myths about self-promotion, so repelled are we by obnoxious braggers, many people simply avoid talking about themselves.'[63]

But I am no expert in this area. I am incredibly hard on myself in the face of failure, as you know by now, but I'm also the last person to give myself a pat on the back if things go well.

Nothing in my working life thus far could compare to the mammoth challenge of writing my first book (well, my second one is right up there in terms of challenges) and the fear that went with it, but when it was published and was warmly received, I was quick to minimise just how much work I had put in. A friend tells me I forget about achievements in the same way women forget how hard it is to give birth – apparently this is nature's way of ensuring they'll happily conceive again. People would comment on the achievement of writing a book – never mind it doing well – and I would say to myself, 'Well, it really wasn't that big a deal and if I could do it, literally anybody could do it', and so on and so forth.

I was uncomfortable with praise. I didn't know what to say in the face of positive feedback because I was afraid of sounding like a dickhead.

The thing is, what you say doesn't just appease other people, it starts to encroach on what you genuinely think about yourself. When I'd done it, and when I'd seen my name on the book and the book on the shelf, I really didn't see it as that big an achievement – and, yes, that is just stupid. Instead, I thought, 'Well, let's see if it does well.' And then it did well. Did I appreciate it then? To an extent, yes, but I wouldn't take credit for it: I told myself and others that I just got lucky or that it was a fluke. Not once, while it was happening, did I reflect and say, 'Well, I put my mind to something and I did it when I thought I couldn't. I'm a good writer and I produced a good book that people are reading.' And then before I knew it, I was right back at my writing desk again, staring down the barrel of book number two, and focusing all my energy on this new, fear-of-failure inducing challenge.

I had adapted too quickly (for which we can blame nature) and belittled my efforts (for which I blame nurture). This discounting of personal achievements, which we replace with more negative things to focus on, is bloody exhausting. Now, we can't do a whole lot about our ability to adapt and we don't need to – it's a very important trait actually – but we can work on how we perceive our success, in the same way we've done work on how we perceive failure.

Why is this important? If you dismiss your achievements, you dismiss your ability and your self-worth. If you're rolling your eyes and waiting for me to quote motivational speaker and life coach Tony Robbins (who, by the way, is a legend and not at all deserving of an eye-roll in my opinion), appreciating success is not just about enjoying life, as it happens, or being in the moment. It's actually about confidence. The thing is, when we take a moment to recognise and appreciate our achievements, no matter how small they may seem, we're proactively building up real self-confidence that will greatly reduce our fear of failure when facing future opportunities. In doing this, we're gaining insights and awareness (that is positive, for a change) that will help us move forward in due time. And, yes, it does make our here and now a lot more enjoyable. If we only hone in on our minor and major cock-ups, imagine what that's going to do to our confidence and our creativity and our motivation? There's a reason why positive affirmations are so commonly used in personal development courses. They work.

This is crucial: acknowledging and appreciating our success and achievements and even our efforts isn't something we do when we already have a full tank of confidence and soaring self-esteem; by doing this all along, we create it.

How to perceive and appreciate success today:

1 First of all, remind yourself that the brain gravitates towards stronger and typically negative emotions, which is why we can recall times we've f*cked up or mistakes we made a lot more easily than their positive counterparts. This is why we have to interrupt the automatic process and refocus.

2 Stop looking for something enormous or hugely significant to celebrate. If we're able to belittle our success when it's big (i.e. passing an exam or publishing a book), you can imagine just how easy it is to overlook the little accomplishments we achieve each day. You need to appreciate the big and the small. And the more you appreciate the small, the more rewarding the big will be. Start by listing five small victories you've had today. It could be ticking a few things off your to-do list or getting that thing off your plate that's been hanging over you. It could be a really satisfying conversation with a best friend over tea.

3 Next, be your own yardstick. To get a sense of how you're doing and to appreciate where you are and to really enjoy the times when you achieve something significant, you need to compare yourself of today with yourself of another time. Rather than comparing yourself to others, because you will always find someone who's ten steps ahead of you, and that will make you feel inadequate.

This is known as 'temporal comparison' and it's very effective (and a lot more helpful than social comparison, which is all about one-upmanship).

If I do this for myself as an example it might be easier to understand. Three years ago, it would have been a major achievement for me to have gone to a shopping centre and come home in one piece without having suffered a panic attack. While I don't want to dwell on the past in any unhelpful way for too long, looking back reminds me of how far I've come. Going out socially and feeling fine may be absolutely nothing to someone else, but for me it's still an achievement today, because of where I was. It's all relative. So I take stock once in a while to remind myself of this growth which bolsters my confidence. Being able to stand up in front of a few hundred people and give a talk may be nothing to someone who talks in front of thousands every day, but for me, given that there was a time I'd rather die than do it, this is a massive achievement. Now, I'm still quick to step down from the podium and say, 'Well, that was nothing', and berate myself for having felt so sick about it in the first place, but I have to consciously interrupt this and appreciate that I did it and pushed through my comfort zone. It's not about anyone else's achievements or anyone else's comfort zone (because everyone's is different), it's about me and mine alone.

4 According to Jack Canfield, author of the bestselling book and phenomenon *Chicken Soup for the Soul*, it's a good idea to create a log book each day of your successes.[64] This is not a gratitude diary as such (which I've always found a bit airy-fairy) but a record each day of the small victories and, of course, the bigger ones. When we give ourselves permission to toot our own horn, we stop craving it from other people. Canfield says that by writing this down every day – and it can be as simple as bullet points – you're recording it in your long-term memory and shifting the balance in favour of the positive. This can become a source of motivation and positive reminders when you're feeling down, but it's also very helpful to review when you find yourself faced with a new challenge. Canfield also recommends recording your achievements to date, starting from when you were very young.

5 Canfield also suggests that you get sentimental with your successes. Gather mementos of positive experiences – photos, medals, anything that alludes to some achievement – and have them readily accessible. When your environment reminds you of your successes, it boosts your confidence and motivates you forward. Currently, I have a few copies of my book and cutouts of articles I've had published dotted around my home office. It helps to visualise my achievements.

As and when you achieve something – significant to you, not to anybody else, remember – have an action plan for taking stock.

6 If it's a biggie, take five minutes (at least) to think about what you've just achieved and remember how you got there. Maybe it's the end result or maybe it's one stepping stone on the road to a bigger goal.

7 Tell yourself and someone close to you that you're proud of what you've achieved. Hearing the words out loud when they come from yourself lodges it into your brain.

8 Accept compliments. When somebody takes the trouble to tell you that you've done a good job, they're usually being honest. You don't have to respond and say, 'I know, I'm amazing, aren't I?', but rejecting a compliment isn't doing you any favours. Believe what you're being told. I find simply saying, 'Thank you so much, that's very kind of you, that's so nice to hear', or something to that effect is a good enough response in that it's accepting of someone's praise and easy enough to say without feeling too uncomfortable.

9 Treat yourself. Give yourself a day or a weekend of indulgence. And be sure to reward not just results but significant effort too. This might be taking your foot off the gas for one day or binge-watching your favourite show without the added guilt or treating yourself to something new you've wanted for ages. This is one thing I am good at.

If you don't reward yourself for a job well done, you run the risk of burnout later on and lost perspective of where you're at. Figure out your own reward system and break your bigger final goals down into smaller goals. When you build rewards into your pursuit of success along the way – as opposed to just at the end – you not only enjoy it more but feel more motivated to move forward. In fact, now that I've successfully completed this chapter (one smaller goal that contributes towards the bigger goal of the finished book), I'm going to take a forty-minute Netflix break with a cup of tea and my feet up on the couch. When I return to the next task at hand, I will be fresher, more motivated and ready.

The Final Tool – Knowing Your Limitations

A WORD OF WARNING: If you take on everything in this confidence kit at once, you will be exhausted. Go easy on yourself.

Personal development is hard bloody work. It's not something you can read about and become an expert on overnight – I am in no way, shape or form an expert myself and have a lot still to learn. Self-growth is something that requires lifelong effort (otherwise there'd only be one book about it and we'd all have it sussed). It's the hardest work you'll ever do, in fact.

But here's what's very important: knowing when to work at it and when to give yourself a break. Knowing what works for you and discarding what doesn't. Everything that's in this book works for me and is based on my own experience, but there is so much out there that doesn't. And I've given up putting myself under pressure for not being the person who makes a seven a.m. yoga class and finds that her confidence soars because of it. For example, if you read my first book, you'll know I'm sh*t at meditation but I count watching *Say Yes To The Dress* in my PJs among my own mindfulness tools. It's about whatever works for you, but I hope there will be some key takeaways from this book that will give you some food for thought or at least put a pep in your step.

On our quest to overcome fear and increase our confidence, it's crucial to accept that we have limits and it's not always a good idea to push right through them. It's just not realistic or sustainable to live a life that's always limitless and fearless. In fact, knowing your limits is, in itself, an essential tool for self-growth. It's just as important as persistence and learning from mistakes.

That's not to say they are permanent limits – they might be things you can do at a later stage – but it's far more beneficial to take it step by step so that your confidence can build at a pace that can be sustained. In fact, if you're interested in personal development, your limits will always be changing, so you'll have to be mindful of them as you go through life. (However, there will never be more than twenty-four hours in a day, so that's one limit that's staying put.) Persistence is necessary because it helps us to reach our limits. Learning from our mistakes is hugely significant as it helps to push our limits the next time around. And knowing that you have limits helps you maximise the return, keeping your wellbeing in check. Think again of the gym analogy: You lift weights and tear your muscles. Your muscles then repair and are stronger. The heavier weights you lift, the more you progress – but there's a flipside to this. If you lift weights that you are not yet ready to lift, you injure yourself and put your progress on hold. Your goal is to make incremental progress, bit by bit, rather than biting off more than you can cope with and winding up worse for wear. It's here that the failures we want so much to avoid can happen.

At this point, it's a good idea to revisit Chapter 1 about the comfort zone and remind yourself that consistently pushing yourself outside of your comfort zone, launching yourself from the frying pan into the fire (going from the learning zone to the potential panic zone) without some downtime in between, won't get you where you want to be. It will be counterproductive and potentially harmful.

Sometimes, you need to allow yourself to say no, and allow yourself to deal with things on another day.

You need to not punish yourself if you give one challenge a miss. Your comfort zone has its importance too and you should respect it. But you'll know when to push yourself and test your limits and when not to. Only you can know that. An honest account of reasons for and against doing something usually helps if you're unclear at first.

What's more, something might seem like a good idea on its own, but you need to take the context into consideration. For example, if I've been asked to give two separate talks, one on a Monday and the other on a Friday, both of which will require enormous energy and take a lot out of me, do I really want to add an additional challenge in for the Wednesday? It might be a good opportunity on its own, but it might be better for me to use the time in between the others to prep, to rest up, to let the hormones involved in fear and confidence settle, before taking on another challenge. Adding a third challenge to the mix might bring me more stress than valuable progress. The mental fatigue of doing that much self-work in such a short space time might lower my limits. That's not to say there won't come a time when I can give five presentations in one week, but for now, this is where I'm at and that's okay. I'm doing fine. So while personal development is important, it's also important that you give yourself a break.

Knowing when to say no, and opting in and out of what suits you, is one of the smartest things you can learn to do.

What is also crucial is watching out for the sticky trap that social comparison can be. For any of this to work for you – or anything you ever read about personal development – you must hone in on yourself alone. The wellness industry has become enormously popular over the past decade. It was great in one sense that we had more awareness about looking after ourselves, physically and mentally. But it had its downsides too. I myself fell into a trap of feeling under pressure to better myself at the same rate as everybody else I was reading about, which defeats the whole purpose. It wasn't just about being nice to yourself or tips on how to nail mindfulness, it became pushy, almost. It became another metric for social comparison, made all the worse by social media. (How often – on Instagram in particular – does something that starts out as motivation turn into a negative spiral of comparing yourself to other people?)

The antidote to our stressful lives, it seems, is now becoming part of the problem. For example, I might find myself thinking, 'I'm stressed out if I haven't done something every day that scares me' because I see other people take on challenges more frequently, or 'I said I'd get five minutes of mindfulness every day and I've missed the last two days', when I see someone else post a selfie in their lotus position. Every day, there could easily be a hundred new articles filled with ten ways you're living life the wrong way (albeit masked as ten ways to self-improve). To be winning at life in every sense we even had to go so far as to arrange our porridge to look like a work of art in a bowl. Nah. No, thank you.

So while, yes, this book is filled with exercises and tools and strategies, it's written for the times when you need it. It's not something to make you feel bad about yourself on a daily basis. And it's not an aggressive call to action demanding that you confront every single fear you've ever had right now and push yourself to the pants-wetting point of panic.

Everyone will be reading this book at different stages. Some of you might be searching for the confidence to cope in a social situation. Others might be looking for the confidence to take a multimillion dollar chance on a business venture (please, do not hunt me down if it doesn't work out for you). So take the tools and strategies that speak to you and apply them to your own situation. You don't need to reach the conclusion of this book and be ready to follow in the steps of JK Rowling (but that's not to say you don't have that potential).

We all operate at different levels, with different markers for our respective comfort zones and different goals that we want to reach. Don't concern yourself with anybody else, that's none of your business, and remember what the stoics said, 'It's beyond your control.' Focus on where you are right now, what you can control and where you want to be. Live within the manageable portions of one day at a time. Do what I do: take the bits that work for you and ignore the rest. I won't be offended (well, I probably will, but then I'll just read up on stoicism some more).

Endnotes

[1] Z. Ziglar, *Over the Top*.

[2] For more information on the Yerkes-Dodson Law see: http://psychclassics.yorku.ca/Yerkes/Law/.

[3] J. Panicucci (2007), 'Cornerstones of Adventure Education', in D. Prouty, J. Panicucci and R. Collinson (eds), *Adventure Education: Theory and Applications* (Champaign, IL: Human Kinetics), pp. 33-48.

[4] L. Leotti, S. Iyengar and K. Ochsner, 'Born To Choose', *Trends in Cognitive Sciences*, vol. 14, no.10, pp. 457-63.

[5] Drs A. and T. Leonard-Curtin, interview with authors, 24 January 2018.

[6] Dr S. Lynch, interview with author, 21 January 2018.

[7] Drs A. and T. Leonard-Curtin, interview with authors, 24 January 2018.

[8] Ibid.

[9] Dr S. Heshmat, interview with author, 24 January 2018.

[10] Drs A. and T. Leonard-Curtin, interview with authors, 24 January 2018.

[11] Ibid.

[12] Dr S. Heshmat, interview with author, 24 January 2018.

[13] S.P. Edwards (2005), 'The Amygdala: The Body's Alarm Circuit', http://www.dana.org/Publications/Brainwork/Details.aspx?id=43615.

[14] Dr I. Gargan, interview with author, 3 November 2017.

[15] I. Pavlov, *Conditioned Reflexes*.

[16] J. Watson and R. Rayner (1920), 'Conditioned Emotional Reactions', *Journal of Experimental Psychology*, vol. 3, no. 1, pp. 1-14. See also: http://psychclassics.yorku.ca/Watson/emotion.htm.

[17] T. Ito, J. Larson, N.K. Smith and J. Cacioppo (1998), 'Negative Information Weighs More Heavily on the Brain: The Negativity Bias in Evaluative Categorizations', *Journal of Personality* and Social Psychology, vol.75, no. 4, pp. 887-900.

[18] 'Overcoming Fear of Failure' Mind Tools: https://www.mindtools.com/pages/article/fear-of-failure.htm.

[19] Y.N. Harari, Sapiens: *A Brief History of Humankind*.

[20] Dr A. and T. Leonard-Curtin, interview with authors, 24 January 2018.

[21] M. Tyrrell, interview with author, 13 December 2017.

[22] 'Elon Musk: How To Build the Future', Y Combinator: https://www.ycombinator.com/future/elon/

[23] A. Cuddy (2012), 'Your Body Language May Shape Who You Are', TED Talks.

[24] G. Desvaux, S. Devillard-Hoellinger and M. Meaney (2008), 'A Business Case for Women', *The McKinsey Quarterly*.

[25] Dr N. Burton (2015), *Heaven and Hell: The Psychology of Emotions*.

[26] M. Tyrrell, interview with author, 13 December 2017.

[27] A. Huffington (2014), *Thrive*.

[28] S. Covey (1989), *The Seven Habits of Highly Effective People*.

[29] D. Cvencek, A.G. Greenwald and A.N. Meltzoff (2016), 'Implicit Measures for Preschool Children Confirm Self-esteem's Role in Maintaining a Balanced Identity', *Journal of Experimental Social Psychology*, no. 62, pp. 50-7.

[30] J. Stoeber and K. Otto (2006), 'PositiveConceptions of Perfectionism: Approaches, Evidence, Challenges', *Personality and Social Psychology Review*, no. 10, pp. 295-319.

[31] M. Tyrrell, interview with author, 13 December 2017.

[32] J. Moser, J. Slane, S.A. Burt andK. Klump, 'Etiologic Relationships Between Anxiety and Dimensions of Maladaptive Perfectionism inYoung Adult Female Twins':https://scholars.opb.msu.edu/en/publications/etiologic-relationships-between-anxiety-and-dimensions-of-maladap-4.

[33] M. Antony and R. Swinson *When Perfect Isn't Good Enough: Strategies for Coping with Perfectionism*.

[34] M. Antony (2013), 'Comprehensive-Treatment of Perfectionism'.

[35] M. Tyrrell, 'Uncommon Knowledge': https://www.unk.com/blog/treating-perfectionism-3-therapy-strategies/.

[36] Ibid.

[37] https://www.express.co.uk/life-style/life/773736/what-is-imposter-syndrome-definition.

[38] P.R. Clance and S. Imes, 'TheImpostor Phenomenon in High-Achieving Women': http://www.paulineroseclance.com/pdf/ip_high_achieving_women.pdf.

[39] S. Sandberg (2013), *Lean In*.

[40] K. Kay and C. Shipman, *The Confidence Code*.

[41] P.R. Clance and S. Imes, 'The Impostor Phenomenon in High-Achieving Women': http://www.paulineroseclance.com/pdf/ip_high_achieving_women.pdf.

[42] Ibid.

[43] C. Cauterucci, 'We Expect Women to Have Impostor Syndrome. That's Why We Can't Handle Hilary Clinton', *Slate* (2016)

[44] For the Dunning-Kruger effect, see: *Journal of Personality and Social Psychology*, vol. 77, no. 6 (December 1999),pp. 1121-34.

[45] R. Holiday (2016), *The Daily Stoic*.

[46] Ibid.

[47] M. Pigliucci (2017), *How to be a Stoic*.

[48] 'Overcoming Fear of Failure' Mind Tools: https://www.mindtools.com/pages/article/fear-of-failure.htm.

[49] Dr S. Peters (2012), *The Chimp Paradox*.

[50] For UCLA study, see: K. Kircanski etal. (2012), 'Feelings into Words: Contributionsof Language to Exposure Therapy', *Psychological Science*, vol. 23, no. 10, pp. 1086-91.

[51] R. Templar (2006), *The Rules of Life*.

[52] K. Milkman, 'Temptation Bundling', see Freakonomics podcast, 'When Willpower Isn't Enough'.

[53] Ibid.

[54] K. Milkman, J.A. Minson and K.G.M. Volpp (2013), 'Holding the HungerGames Hostage at the Gym', *Management Science*, vol. 60, no. 2, pp. 283-99.

[55] O. Burkeman (2013), *The Antidote: Happiness for People Who Can't Stand Positive Thinking*.

[56] T. Seabourne (2012), *The Complete Idiot'sGuide To Quick Total Body Workouts*.

[57] T. Kraft and S. Pressman (2012), 'Grin and Bear It: The Influence of Manipulated Positive Facial Expression on the Stress Response', *Psychological Science*, vol. 23, no. 11, pp. 1372-1378

[58] A. Cuddy, D. Carney and A. Yap (2010),'Power Posing: Brief Nonverbal Displays Affect Neuroendocrine Levels and Risk Tolerance', *Psychological Science*, vol. 21, no. 10, pp. 1363-8.

[59] H. Adam and A.D. Galinsky (2012),'Enclothed Cognition', *Journal of Experimental Social Psychology*, vol. 48, no. 4, pp. 918-25.

[60] M. Tyrrell, interview with author, 13 December 2017.

[61] J. Wise, *Psychology Today* article: https://www.psychologytoday.com/blog/extreme-fear/201303/how-real-life-change-happens.

[62] Dr N. Ramlakhan (2011), *Tired But Wired: How To Overcome Your SleepProblems*.

[63] P. Klaus (2003), *Brag: The Art of TootingYour Own Horn Without Blowing It*.

[64] J. Canfield (2013), *Chicken Soup for the Soul*.

Bibliography

Books

Antony, Martin and Swinson, Richard (2009), *When Perfect Isn't Good Enough: Strategies for Coping with Perfectionism* (Oakland, CA: New Harbinger Publications).

Burkeman, Oliver (2013), *The Antidote: Happiness for People Who Can't Stand Positive Thinking* (London: Faber & Faber).

Burton, Dr Neel (2015), *Heaven and Hell: The Psychology of Emotions* (Oxford: Acheron Press).

Covey, Stephen (1989), *The Seven Habits of Highly Effective People* (London: Simon & Schuster UK Ltd).

Canfield, Jack (2013), *Chicken Soup for the Soul* (20th Anniversary edition) (Cos Cob, CT: Chicken Soup for the Soul Publishing).

Harari, Yuval Noah (2014), *Sapiens: A Brief History of Humankind* (London: Random House Ltd).

Harris, Russ (2011), *The Confidence Gap* (London: Robinson).

Holiday, Ryan (2016), *The Daily Stoic* (New York: Random House). See also: website address].

Huffington, Ariana (2014), *Thrive* (London: Penguin Books).

Kay, Katty and Shipman, Claire (2014), *The Confidence Code* (New York: Harper-Collins).

Klaus, Peggy (2003), *Brag: The Art of Tooting Your Own Horn Without Blowing It* (New York: Warner Business Book).

Pavlov, Ivan (1927), *Conditioned Reflexes: An Investigation of the Physiological Activity of the Cerebral Cortex* (Oxford: Oxford University Press).

Peters, Dr Steve (2012), *The Chimp Paradox* (London: Random House).

Puigliucci, Massimo (2017) *How To Be a Stoic* (London: Rider).

Ramlakhan, Dr Nerina (2011), *Tired But Wired: How To Overcome Your Sleep Problems* (London: Souvenir Press).

Sandberg, Sheryl (2013), *Lean In* (New York: Alfred A. Knopf).

Seabourne, Tom (2012), *The Complete Idiot's Guide To Quick Total Body Workouts* (New York: Penguin Random House).

Templar, Richard (2006), *The Rules of Life* (London: Pearson Education).

Ziglar, Zig (1997), *Over the Top: Moving from Survival to Stability, from Stability to Success, from Success to Significance* (Edinburgh: Thomas Nelson Publishers).

Journals

Kruger, J. and Dunning, D. (1999), 'Unskilled and Unaware of It', *Journal of Personality and Social Psychology*, vol. 77, no. 6, pp. 1121-34.

Adam, H. and Galinsky, A.D. (2012),'Enclothed Cognition', *Journal of Experimental Social Psychology*, vol. 48, no. 4, pp. 918-25.

Clance, P.R. and Imes, S. 'TheImpostor Phenomenon in High-Achieving Women': http://www.paulineroseclance.com/pdf/ip_high_achieving_women.pdf.

Desvauz, G., Devillard-Hoellinger, S. and Meaney, M. (2008), 'A Business Case forWomen', *The McKinsey Quarterly*.

Ito, T., Larson, J., Smith, N.K. and Cacioppo, J. (1998), 'Negative Information Weighs More Heavily on the Brain:The Negativity Bias in Evaluative Categorizations', *Journal of Personalityand Social Psychology*, vol.75, no. 4, pp. 887-900.

Kircanski, K. et al. (2012), 'Feelings into Words: Contributions of Language to Exposure Therapy', *Psychological Science*, vol. 23, no. 10, pp. 1086-91.

Leotti, L, Iyengar, S. and Ochsner, K., 'Born To Choose', *Trends in Cognitive Sciences*, vol. 14, no.10, pp. 457-63

Milkman, K., Minson, J.A. and Volpp, K.G.M. (2013), 'Holding the Hunger Games Hostage at the Gym', *Management Science*, vol. 60, no. 2, pp. 283-99.

Moser, J., Slane, J., Burt, S.A. and Klump, K., 'Etiologic Relationships Between Anxiety and Dimensions of Maladaptive Perfectionism in Young Adult Female Twins':https://scholars.opb.msu.edu/en/publications/etiologic-relationships-between-anxiety-and-dimensions-of-maladap-4.

Panicucci, J. (2007), 'Cornerstones of Adventure Education', in D. Prouty, J. Panicucci and R. Collinson (eds), *Adventure Education: Theory and Applications* (Champaign,IL: Human Kinetics), pp. 33-48.

Stoeber, J. and Otto, K. (2006), 'Positive Conceptions of Perfectionism: Approaches, Evidence, Challenges', *Personality and Social Psychology Review*, no. 10, pp. 295-319.

Watson, J. and Rayner, R. (1920), 'Conditioned Emotional Reactions', *Journal of Experimental Psychology*, vol. 3, no. 1, pp. 1-14. See also: http://psychclassics.yorku.ca/Watson/emotion.htm

Websites

http://psychclassics.yorku.ca/Yerkes/Law/http://www.dana.org/Publications/Brainwork/Details.aspx?id=43615.

https://science.howstuffworks.com/life/inside-the-mind/emotions/fear6.htm

http://psycnet.apa.org/doiLanding?doi=10.1037%2F0097-7403.29.4.323

https://www.ycombinator.com/future/elon/

https://www.sciencedirect.com/science/article/pii/S0022103115001250

https://www.unk.com/blog/treating-perfectionism-3-therapy-strategies/

https://www.mindtools.com/pages/article/fear-of-failure.htm

http://www.slate.com/blogs/xx_factor/2016/03/28/impostor_syndrome_is_expected_of_women_but_hillary_clinton_won_t_conform.html

Interviews with the Author

Drs Aisling and Trish Leonard-Curtin

Dr Sinead Lynch

Dr Shahram Heshmat

Dr Ian Gargan

Mark Tyrrell

Acknowledgements

Everyone listed here has, in their own way, been instrumental in the building and maintaining of my own confidence as I put this kit together. While it's not included as a tool within the book, surrounding yourself with decent people gets an honorary mention; it makes a huge difference to have people in your life who can see your potential and encourage you to move forward, when you're drunk on a cocktail of self-doubt.

Thank you to my editor Ciara Doorley at Hachette for giving me the opportunity to write another book. And holding my hand through the editing process which you know I loathe entirely. Thank you to Joanna Smyth, also with Hachette, for the million and one things you do. Thank you to Alan Keane, who looks after the book publicity and forces me out of my comfort zone (and onto live TV sets); he has been there for most of my 'stretch-zone experiences', and plenty of lovely brunches too. Thank you to Faith my literary agent for all of your support and words of wisdom. Thank you Cathal O'Gara for yet another beauty of a cover.

Thank you to a select few ass-kicking female friends who have talked me through many a meltdown. Jo, you are my career partner in crime and my biggest cheerleader. I would not be where I am without you. Aileen, Laura, Una, Nikki, Niamh D, Sandra and Niamh K – I don't know what I'd do without you and our lowbrow conversations. Melanie – another cheerleader I'm proud to have by my side. Cara Doyle – thank you in particular for making me feel like a queen when I need to. Louise O'Neill, how lucky I am to now call you a friend and have your incredibly generous advice on the other end of the phone. Megan O'Riordan, the same goes for you, you legend and female powerhouse. And you, Valerie Roe. And you, Alison Curtis and Jennifer Rock. Thank you to the men too: Bressie, you are so kind and encouraging and you never bullsh*t me. Dave O, you keep me grounded and delightfully immature. Alan gets a second mention as a friend and not just a professional acquaintance.

Thank you to my mother, Aideen, who has the patience of a saint and helped me get through the dotting of all the *is* and crossing of all the *ts* in the final stages of the book. I'm so grateful to her for her quality control; she could easily say everything I do is 'amazing' because I am her daughter, but she knows I want to create something that's actually good. Thanks to you and Dad – Tony, for always supporting me and loving me and letting me resort to a state of childlike dependency when things in life go tits-up. Thank you Daniel, my brother, for making way more of an effort with the FaceTime chats – I promise to be better – and for all your podcast and book recommendations. You're a one-of-a-kind big brother.

Thank you to Barry, who I will soon call my husband (must read the fear-hacking chapter again; just kidding). You are the greatest thing in my life. Thank you for cooking me dinner every night because I'm 'too tired' (read = too lazy) from writing this book. Thanks for showing an active interest in every single chapter as it came together and giving me the feedback I needed. Thanks for loving me (and all of my other personalities). Thanks to your family too – Hazel, Des and Ian – for minding our fur baby Bear when I've taken off on a 'writer's retreat', and keeping every one of my press clippings.

Finally, thank you to the fans of *Owning It*, from all corners of the globe (excuse me while my head inflates), who went out of their way to send me messages detailing how helpful they found the book and how it was just what they needed at a sh*t time and how they recommended it to a friend or a family member. I am eternally grateful and so humbled. I never expected any of this. Because of all of you, and the incredible feedback you continue to give me, I felt capable of producing another book. Thanks to you, dear reader, for picking up this book. I hope you enjoy it and, most of all, if you've just gotten to the end of the book, I hope it's made a difference to your confidence.

X Caroline

Read on for an extract from
*Owning It: Your Bullsh*t-Free
Guide to Living with Anxiety*
by Caroline Foran

Introduction

This whole idea of 'curing' your anxiety so that you never have to feel it again – which plenty of books out there claim to do, preying on your vulnerability – only serves to make you feel worse in the long run.

DISCLAIMER: The first and perhaps most important point you can take from the following 250 or so pages is that I am not in any way, shape or form a healthcare professional. I don't have a degree in psychology nor do I have any qualifications that would otherwise allow me to make specific recommendations to you on how to deal with the veritable sh*t show that is your current experience of anxiety. However, now that you've bothered to pick up this book, here's what I *can* offer: experience and empathy (as well as a whole lotta research).

ANOTHER DISCLAIMER: Sticking to the title's promise of keeping this as bullsh*t free as possible, the truth is, this book won't 'cure' your anxiety. I'm sorry; you probably hated reading that; you just want to feel better – like yesterday – and I understand that, I did too. But here's something you might not have heard before; this whole idea of 'curing' your anxiety so that you never have to feel it again – which plenty of books out there claim to do, preying on your vulnerability – only serves to make you feel worse in the long run. Watch out for that; I wasted a small fortune chasing quick fixes and sensationalist claims.

What you *will* get from this book is the understanding voice of someone who's felt as crap as you do now and, like you, has no time for BS or overly technical jargon that makes everything sound a whole lot more scary than it needs to be. Anxiety, by its very nature, is disconcerting enough; this book aims to keep things simple and break down what anxiety is so that you can regain control.

The main aim of this book – and what I want to get you thinking about before we dive right in – is the idea of OWNING your anxiety so that it no longer impacts negatively on your life.

This book is about changing your relationship with your anxiety. Though your instincts right now are telling you otherwise, the key is not to resist it. Not to run a million miles away from it. Not to cure it. But to learn the art of managing it.

Anxiety is something we will all encounter at some point in our lives, some of us just feel it more than others. As for those whom you look at enviously, wondering how they go through life so seemingly carefree, perhaps it will be just a matter of time before anxiety rears its ugly head for them too – or maybe they're already feeling it on the inside and you just don't know it.

You see, there's no stereotypical or easily identifiable anxiety sufferer. We don't walk around breathing erratically into brown paper bags or set our Facebook status to 'anxious' for all the world to see. Though it's far from the upbeat perspective you're looking for, stress and anxiety are nearly impossible to avoid in the twenty-first century, and the last thing I want to do is tell you how to live a stress-free and anxiety-free life. I tried that, as many have, but it doesn't work; it's futile. You just end up feeling frustrated and more anxious, and all that improves is your self-help book collection.

Thankfully, though, what is possible is managing anxiety and, better still, making it work for you, whatever your age.

Throughout *Owning It: Your Bullsh*t-Free Guide To Living With Anxiety*, I will chronicle my own experience of anxiety – a lot of which you'll no doubt recognise in yourself – and I will share the most practical and positive tools that can help you feel like you again. When you're right in the thick of it or plummeting deep down into the abyss, which is how a bad bout of anxiety can feel, it's hard to imagine that there'll ever be a time when you won't feel untethered or unable to cope. My aim here is to reassure you that you will. You'll fly it.

So, you're probably wondering, now that I no longer feel defined by my anxiety – or the need to introduce myself with a warning, like: 'Hello, I'm an anxious person and I might, at any moment, burst into flames' – why would I want to drag it all up again? Why don't I just go on living my life to the fullest without giving too much oxygen to a bad experience? The thing is, I know for sure that my own anxiety wouldn't have been anywhere near as traumatic if I had known then what I know now. And with so many people starting to come out of the woodwork and admit that they, too, don't feel so good, I want to share my learnings – good and bad – so that you can also pull yourself out of that initial black hole of despair and learn to cope. Most importantly, though, I want to be honest and to the point, as I believe this will save you time, money and any further, unnecessary suffering.

You see, when my anxiety hit me like a big fat freight train that I just did not see coming, I was desperate to talk to someone who *wasn't* a professional. For me, 'professionals' were people who were incredibly well read and qualified on the subject, but who lacked any real empathetic insight into just how shi**y I was feeling. When I felt like my world had come crashing down for no good reason, I wanted to see proof of a real, live, functioning human being who underneath it all.

I say that you'll never have to go through this again because it's true, and not because it sounds like something contrived that you'll find on Pinterest with a swirly font. It's very hard to convince yourself of this when you feel like you're all but losing your mind, but get familiar with this idea now. Someday soon, you'll wish you could go back in time and reassure yourself of this inevitability. Sometimes, even now (because I'm still human), I think: 'My anxiety took me completely off guard before, and I fell apart, who's to say that won't happen again?' And then I stop myself: I can never, not for the rest of my life, be taken by surprise by anxiety and fall entirely victim to its power.

Today, I know too much. I understand it entirely. I now accept that I'm a sensitive creature who feels things a little more than the person next to me might, and I'm okay with that.

I recognise the signs and the symptoms of anxiety, I know how to manage them and, not only am I able to put out fires as they arise, I can prevent the fires from arising by taking really good care of myself.

Though I've got a good handle on it (well you'd certainly hope so, now that you've bought this book), I don't consider myself to be particularly enlightened. I did not, unfortunately, have an *Eat Pray Love* kind of epiphany. I did not go to Bali and meet an all-seeing, toothless medicine man who schooled me in the art of living in the here and now (but hey, that might help) and I'm still not particularly good at meditation. I still have sh*tty, stressful work days, or days when I feel a little below par – one day when I was particularly exhausted, ratty and hormonal, I cried because my boyfriend ate my last chicken nugget – but that, dear reader, is the human experience, whether you're eighteen, twenty-eight or sixty-eight. What I have now, however, is a quiet confidence in myself to pull through the speed bumps and curveballs that life is sure to throw, thanks to the arsenal of effective tools that I keep tucked under my imaginary yellow umbrella. No matter how big the raincloud, I know now that it will pass. But there was a long time where I was never sure if it would.

So, let's talk about what this book can do for you. Rather than give you one giant mountain of reading to dive into – the prospect of which might just be enough to give you anxiety – this book is structured in two very simple parts that mirror how I strongly suggest you approach your own situation. For me, it's a tried-and-tested technique that I return to anytime I feel even the slightest bit wobbly. Even if you're feeling particularly woeful, just knowing that you've got a plan of action will give you the reassurance that all is not lost. So, let's get to it: first we *assess*, then we *address*.

Assess *(Or as I like to call it, the What-the-f*ck-is-going-on? part of the book)*

Beyond your own set of circumstances, you first need to understand what anxiety is, how it functions, why we feel it, why so many of us experience it, and why the presence of stress or anxiety in our bodies is actually nothing to worry about. You also need to wrap your head around something known as the 'negativity bias'. At first, it might seem like there's an awful lot of information to absorb, but don't be overwhelmed. This is a good thing; it means there are several ways through the fog and you're not destined for a life defined by anxiety. Take comfort in that.

Lest we forget, knowledge is power. Having a firm grasp of exactly what anxiety is and precisely why you're feeling it is half the battle. It really is. Most of my own suffering was born from not having the faintest clue about what was going on, an unwillingness to address why I was feeling it (out of fear, naturally) and just totally panicking about the fact that I was panicking, which, as you can imagine, was a fairly self-perpetuating quandary.

Before you throw the kitchen sink at your anxiety or trawl the internet in a blind panic for that one quick fix upon which you so desperately hope to stumble (please, resist the urge), you have to take stock of your current situation and the events that have led you here. What's going on? Did it really come out of the blue? How long have you been feeling this way? What's happening in your life, e.g. relationships, exams at school, pressure at work? Now I'm not suggesting you answer each of these questions right here this second, otherwise the first part of this book would be rendered unnecessary. Together, we'll paint a clear picture.

Address *(Or, the What-the-f*ck-am-I-going-to-do-about-it? part of the book)*

When you've done the work of part one, and success-fully assessed your situation, we will move swiftly on to the art of addressing it.

The first time you educate yourself about anxiety is always the toughest because it's when you tend to feel the worst and the most overwhelmed, but when you've got a general understanding of it, it's then a matter of assessing individual bouts of anxiety as they arise, and eventually you'll get really good at saying, 'Oh yes, I can see why I feel this way, that makes total sense', before employing the specific anti-anxiety tools that you know will work for you.

Within this section of the book, with the help of some incredibly qualified advocates of the bullsh*t-free approach to giving you the information you need, we'll explore everything from what you put into your body to the many treatment options and tools that are available to you. Instead of attacking your anxiety like the enemy, we'll work with it, dealing with both the physical and the emotional symptoms on the one-way road to Owning It.

Throughout the book, you will also find a wealth of practical exercises to get stuck into, all of which were a huge help to me (and still are). Some of these exercises have been formulated with the help of Dr Malie Coyne, clinical psychologist, while others are tried-and-tested favourites from some of the most helpful online resources.

My advice to you, before you go any further, is to pick up a journal or a copybook of some sort, so that you can get to work with the exercises as you read through this book. Putting pen to paper will make a huge difference; you'll feel instantly empowered for having taken over the reins of your anxiety and you'll find it far easier to keep track of and notice your progress on the road to owning it. If this feels futile at first – it did for me – keep at it. I promise it will help.

Between Parts 1 and 2, you'll find a series of quick and easy chapters that you can jump to any time you feel the need. These include my ultimate panic attack rescue guide, which will walk you through those particularly hairy moments, fifteen easy things you can do for your anxiety today, my anxiety survival kit and plenty more.

On the whole, I've structured this book in such a way that you can dip in and out as you please; it doesn't have to be devoured in one go from cover to cover – and you can (and should!) return to the chapters that resonate most with you as often as you can. Keep it handy, throw it in your bag when you're on the go, and consider it your ultimate go-to whether you're feeling a little overwhelmed, you're right in the grip of a petrifying panic attack or whether you've been suffering below the surface for quite some time. Wherever you find yourself on the spectrum from carefree to anxious mess (I was certainly closer to the latter), you will find something within these pages that speaks to you.

So, without further ado, Part 1, Chapter 1: What is anxiety?

Owning It by Caroline Foran is available in print and on ebook now.